Holding Onto Somewhere

by

W. Kay Shabazz

 Published by Carbon2Diamond Press 191 Schofield Drive Whitehall, Ohio 43213. www.Carbon2DiamondPress.com

Library of Congress Cataloging-in-Publication Data
Library of Congress Control Number: 2011901279
W.Kay Shabazz

978-0-615-43567-1
ISBN 10-061543567X

Cover design by Larry Hamill and R. Berry @ One Jah Studio

Dedication

This book is dedicated to the lion, the panther & the Pisces. Your courageous heart, your relentless determination & your nurturing love are testaments to God's infinite power—live His purpose.

Acknowledgements

Thank you God for turning burdens into a blessings, for not giving up on me when I gave up on myself, and working it out in better ways than I could even imagine.

The boys; the world is yours if you work hard and continue to live in Him.
Basir, March 2005 confirmation of God's love for me, when I met you. Thank you for all you have given me since.

My girls: SAVIOR; girls in God are unstoppable!

Introduction

It is the place where ancestors went in mind's eye following flat seas and North Stars. Where people in chains, backs whipped, plantation raped, bought, sold, gassed & trafficked have gone to play and sing songs. Prisoners and pipe smokers leave dark cells and alley ways to spend time there holding loved ones. Little girls get there over rainbows and little boys through crowded stadiums. Now moments flash across plasma screens and IMAX in animation or 3-D, and reality is edited. These days there always looks better than here and there has more coveters than connectors. It is a place as unique as the person who strives to get there. Still, few have been able to imagine themselves here, and when they have seen it, the trip has given them more courage to act than they ever thought possible. People have dumped their baggage, blocking others way. Some have left their trash for others to trip over. There is no baggage fee, but those with excess won't take off. Hold on…

1
Ties That Bind

The whole world stopped as I stood there, my heart broken into tiny pieces that resembled specks on the terrazzo floor that lay beneath. My eyes seemed to be looking at the figure in front of me, a familiar silhouette, but iced over somehow. A voice broke my stupor, "Mom, we…"

I breathed in through my nose, and lowered my eyelids, trying to fill my lungs to capacity with the sweet fragrance of what had been my life source for many years. I could feel the water welling up in my eyes, the inside of my nostrils getting wet, so I swallowed, hoping it would give me a moment before the gates in my eyes opened. I saw my oldest son reaching for my hand. My forehead was sweating, but I could feel my fingertips were cold. I couldn't think of an appropriate gesture for what I was about to do, so I reached into my purse and brought two 1 dollar bills from my wallet. "You keep this baby, and I am going to come back and get it." As I said it my chest jumped as if I couldn't get air. I opened my mouth to breathe, and an 11 carat tear fell from my eye and hung onto my chin.

My youngest son came up and wrapped his arm around my leg "Are you going to stay with us?" Malcolm, the senior of the two, just looked at me quietly, grasping my hand and the money and letting neither of them go. I kneeled down taking each of their faces into my hands, softly analyzing their every feature. "No, baby, I can't stay. I really want to stay with you, but I have to go."

"Then, we want to go with you."

I straightened up and looked at my husband, the man I would follow to the ends of the Earth, and this had been the end of my Earth, the hot tropical sub-Saharan lands of a third world country in Western Africa. He stood there, unmoved and void as he took his hands and slowly pulled the boys towards his body. He didn't have to say a word, and he knew he didn't have to because I was in his country. His country, where women are seen and not heard. Where men, no matter what they had achieved or the paths they had chosen, should never have their judgment questioned by a woman. A country where boys are revered over girls and custody is never an issue. I knew far too well the place I was in.

"I know baby, and I want you to, but your father wants you to stay here with him." I then turned to look into my eldest's eyes, "I need you to promise me that you will watch over your brother. There is a scrap book for you on your desk near your computer with all of my numbers and your great grandfather's address. I love you so much, and never doubt for a minute that you two are not on my mind. I want to be with you, but I can't stay here. I have to go, but I will see you very soon, I promise." I couldn't say another word and be able to contain my pain. The ground was opening up and each piece of my heart was falling inside.

"I will, Mom, and I know."

My son looked at me with quiet understanding, I couldn't express it, but it was the look in his eyes that kept my knees from buckling at that moment. Then, a vulture swept down and grabbed the last piece of my heart as it fell into the Earth. My husband turned them away from me and walked with his arms around the boys, as I stood frozen at that terminal in a sea of my own tears between the Gates 4Him and 2Me. All I wanted to do was to fall to my knees and beg for my children. All I had ever done, working 16 hours a day, protecting that Negro from the drug game. Then watching what pieces of myself I had grown to know disappear in front of my eyes. When I couldn't see my way to stand for myself certainly I could stand for my precious kings, my boys. As their figures grew smaller, my vision became faint from the weight of my tears and my recollection of how I got here.

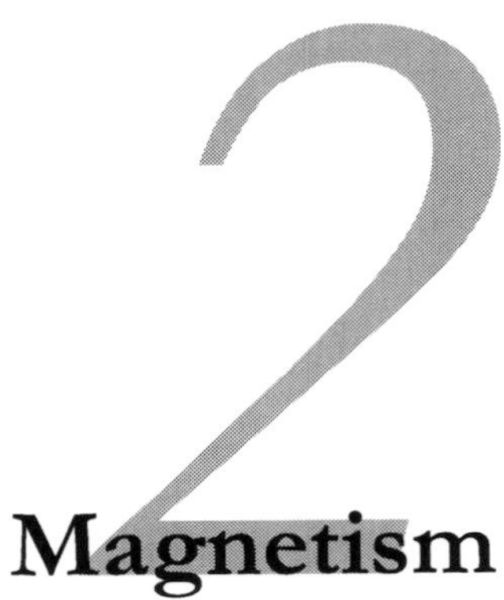

Magnetism

I believe in being down for your man; ride or die, Jay-Z's Bonny and Clyde, from the streets to the sheets, whatever it takes to lift a Black Man up, because he has to work twice as hard to be thought half as good in the world, so he needs a woman who can lift him up at home. I had a gift of encouragement.

I stand five foot seven, shapely size six, with pretty legs like a horse, or at least that's what my husband said when he met me. I was his redbone, shoulder length black hair which frames slender facial features, almond eyes and pouty lips. Gbenga courted me with an enticing mix of humbleness and enthusiasm. To his boys, I was his bitch; loyal like a determined fiery female dog, but gentle like a puppy. But to my face, he called me his queen, a combination of Elizabeth and Amina, he would laugh. More like Sheeba and Saartjie, I would ponder.

When I was coming up I got my "straightenin" from my paternal

Grandmother. I was raised in a Baptist church, and going wasn't optional, I mean every Sunday -all day. I went to Sunday school, Sunday worship, Monday Girls Guild, Wednesday Youth Choir, and all day Saturday, or at least the best part of the day, serving on the Usher Board. I did this routine until I graduated from high school, and when I entered college, I continued doing it, until I moved out from my grandparents' house. It may seem harsh, but I loved my grandmother. She's gone now so I can say confidently she is my hero. It took me a while to realize you shouldn't idolize living heroes because they still have time while they are living to prove you wrong.

My grandparents were married for 64 years until my grandmother died, until death do us part. I admired that. I wanted that same thing one day. My birth parents, on the other hand, were separated. Never divorced, maybe out of respect or holding on to their glory, neither of them would say, but their love could be looked at as a love story or a tragedy. I never had the fortune to be raised by either my natural mother or father, but as I got older their story draped me like a generational curse. I often wondered if the way I learned to love was a forgotten fragment from family?

My father was a hustler, as I got exposed to the "underbelly" of Columbus I found that everybody on the North and Near East side knew of him or his reputation. He had his hand in many a criminal lifestyle, but everyone said the same thing: "He was smart, he thought of crimes that other people looked over." Even people who never worked with him, but knew him when they served time in jail said he knew how to hustle on the inside as well as he knew how to hustle the outside. This amazed me, because my father was not a very intimidating looking man. He was toffee brown, small in frame, a good looking man who stood straight as the boys at West Point, but not what I would see as daunting. He could read an entire room, always finding an angle, but personally he chose to only see through the prism of his own interests.

Gbenga had an equal effect on people he met. Maybe it was the way his eyelids seemed to just rest on his deep brown eyes, or the stride in his walk. He had a commanding presence, though he only stood five foot ten. It could have been the syrupy rasp in his voice or the way he always wore his hats to one side, soft enough to not appear to touch one wave of his hair. It could have even been his impeccable style in clothes: never thuggish, always dapper in tailor- made suits, hangin' from his shoulders, pinstripes aligned at every seam, three point pocket squares and tailored cuffs around his ankles. Gbenga, being from West Africa, resembled Djimon Hounsou; athletic built and chocolate to the bone. He was clever, calculating, but he gripped the American Dream like he was pulling his entire tribe with him.

Enter my mother, a baller, a booster, and an all around "Bonny" for her man. Moms was not always this way. She grew up in the church under a strict West Indian father and a very protective mother. But she was beautiful, a knockout, thin physique with back and all that. She had a flawless rich, glowing coppertone complection, a gorgeous grade of soft deep brown shoulder- length hair and a body that said "pla-dow"! Her almond- shaped soft brown eyes sparkled when she talked, and her charisma made her approachable. Now although I couldn't remember seeing my mother after I had been taken from her at six months old, that smile stretched from her thin lips and the low tones of her voice would creep into my dreams.

A close encounter would bring us back together. I was 17. By this time she had a new boyfriend, a quieter life, but I could see pieces of her strong will and aspirations from the stories I had heard. Some of the pieces in me, were now coming together, many deeper than the familiar reflections we saw standing next to each other.

My father met my mother on Columbus' East Side, he was already deep in "the life" and after the death of her father, spending weekends with a stern Jamaican grandmother and being the oldest child and only girl, she wanted to get away from a life of rearing her younger brothers. She met my father when she was nearly sixteen and he blew her hair back. He showed her a life she never had before and in her he groomed a prize mare, a workhorse, a beautiful woman who would do anything to support her man.

My dad had a strong mouth piece. He convinced my Grandma V to sign the papers so the two of them could get married. My mom earned a reputation for being the hottest booster in town, fur coats, jewelry, designer clothes no knock offs big ticket items. He planned it, she executed, and they stacked the money buying Cadillacs, designer clothes and exquisite furniture. Their connections and reputations in the life got better and deeper and eventually led to selling drugs. When money got good, their habits got bad, and after late parties with contacts, my father got her hooked on dope. For a while, I imagine, that is how he kept her, because after a while she knew she was beautiful and noticed other men thought so too. Momma also noticed that she was not the only honey daddy was getting from the pot. She got scorned, he got popped, she found out she was pregnant. Outside appearances masked another side of Momma when it suited her. She was far from the dreamy girl she was as a teen. To the contrary she was a born strategist and survivor, possessing a calculating mind, a woman who could quickly read a person or situation and then manipulate almost anyone or anything to her advantage. And when necessary, she was able to cut her losses and walk away from any situation without remorse. Somewhere at the end of their story she was stealing some fur coats when a security man approached her, and she was carrying drugs and a gun in her purse. The officer went to grab her, she put the gun to his head and then took off runnin'. The excitement caused her to go into labor and she delivered me in a hospital under the name of an alias and later took me to her mother's house while she lay low. My cries must have kept my Grandma V up all night, because after she tried everything to console me, she took me to a hospital. I didn't go home to see my mom again. I was now in the custody of the state, labeled what some may call now a "crack baby". Outside of our looks some people found it hard to believe Ven was my mother, especially when her raw humor and chic aggressiveness were so different from my understated demeanor.

I don't know, maybe that is where it started with Gbenga and me. Did

I inherit my mom's flavor in relationships? That's what comes across my mind as I try to rationalize it. I was adopted from the hospital, raised in a house in the suburbs, by a white family, as opposite from the 'hood on Livingston and 22nd as one could get. I went to good schools, I was always engaged in my studies, received good grades, was an all-state track runner, graduated to go off to a Big Ten college, but something inside of me was missing.

In the middle of high school I left my adoptive family to move in with my grandparents. It turned out that with all of the ballet classes, the orchestra concerts and modeling scholarships, my new mom still didn't understand that I had no choice but to wake up Black every morning. She thought it was something I could change, like what jeans I put on. She never understood that the older I became, the further my friends from our suburban neighborhood distanced themselves from me. I still liked them, and they spoke to me from the sidewalk or waved to me from their parents' car as they rode down the street. But from somewhere, like a cool wind at the change of summer to fall, my color became a cloak of discontent. Friends always knew I was Black; my color was not fair enough to pass. I was brown enough to be interesting, but not too brown to be offensive. It didn't happen overnight, but as I became a teen they stopped seeing me in my difference, but instead saw me for my difference. So naturally I started making friends with more people who looked like me. My mom, I always called her mom even though she was not my natural mother, didn't take the change so smoothly. She did not want "them" in her house. When I realized, the "them" was me, or at least what made them, "them", was because they looked like me, my relationship with her changed. Mommy never really looked at me as her pretty girl. I was her pretty little Black girl, cut from a tree deeply rooted in culture only to be replanted in a topiary park. I was still a tree. I might have been pruned in the shape of a swan, but my leaves full and lush were attached to branches, that had a trunk and roots which grew deep in rich black soil which supplied nourishment for me to grow. My mom's love was conditional and my dad was conditioned to keep peace with her, so I went to live with my grandparents. I feel that was how I developed my relationships towards men and fell for Gbenga. He appeared to know his identity, so certainly he could help me be secure in mine.

When I met Gbenga I was in my last year of college. From appearances I was doing well. I got good grades, I was a member of a little sister group for one of the divine nine Greek organizations, I had my own apartment, and I had my own small business doing catering and wedding consulting for a lot of my church members. The money was not great but I supported myself and could afford to buy books, pay rent on my small campus apartment, and put gas in my car. I was independent and managing my life. College began to expose me to more culture, introducing me to broaden my thinking, develop my wings. While I studied philosophy and fine art by day, I discovered the fine art of anatomy by night. College seemed to bring out an optimistic panorama in brothers, hopefulness in what lies ahead of them. I became attracted to their intellectual confidence, rather than the physical self found in younger Black men who feel their athletic abilities are the only advantage they have in a system that widely passes over Blacks when referencing academic affairs. I started to see myself more as a woman, with expression and feelings, and less as a machine, using sports and tasks to guard my emotions.

*****

I was shaken by the turbulence, somewhere between Africa and London. The flight attendant came around to me, apparently my eyes were swollen into tiny slits, where just a trace of brown could be seen and the whites of my eyes were now a soft pink from crying so long. She offered me a drink and a warm towel for my face. I thanked her and took it, wondering if she knew the significance of the two empty seats beside me. I could have lain down across them to get more comfortable, my head and ear still swollen and ringing from two days before, but I knew only my children's presence could mend this huge hole in my gut that was filled with loss and loneliness. The word regret never came to my mind, because somehow when children are involved, their birth brings significance to the pain, to the heartache. They were a small reason why I stayed, and the reason why I left.

*****

I was so excited when I found out I was pregnant. It was two weeks before I graduated from college, and I had been dating Gbenga for nearly eight months. What could be a brighter future for a Black child dealing with

America than to have a strong, Black, African father, who understood worldly politics, and never carried the sting from the word Nigger? But something inside of me did not feel right. I thought it was the concern about the timing, I had written requests for a fashion internship at several companies and well-known designer labels, I had an offer to go out and work for a leading hip-hop fashion house out on the West coast, I considered opening up my own restaurant and catering business. I just finished my business plan, life was just opening up when the double line on the E P T test read "pregnant". Not the best timing, but I was excited about having a child of my own. A baby I knew would grow up loved in a two parent home, never sent out for adoption, always knowing love and having a sense of identity.

"Would you name your child Jr. if you had a boy?" I asked as I shifted in my seat.

"No, I would want my child to have their own start, their own identity."

"Well, what if your first child was a girl?"

"Girl or boy, if they look as beautiful as you I don't mind."

In the beginning his words were so sweet and so was his demeanor. He had a confidence in his walk, his movements were so fluid, and his chin just cocked up towards the sky. He had the regality of an African prince, very comfortable in his chocolate skin. A beautiful mouth, his lips so full, I would flutter thinking of their softness against my own. He wasn't chiseled like an athlete, but he was polished mahogany with broad shoulders and an aggressive stance, like he was carrying the majesty and mystery of the Ark in his shoes.

There was a seductive magic packed into his five ten frame, everything about him was African, and I loved it. He was comfortable in himself, he made no excuses for what society gave him and he was willing to work hard to get his own piece of the American dream. I had an admiration for his ambition.

Gbenga settled in Houston among relatives and a large Nigerian population. I really wanted to tell him to his face that I was pregnant. He bought me a ticket to fly to Houston to visit. Gbenga rode with a friend of his to pick me up at the airport. The whole ride I did nothing but look out the window, knowing that my luggage was not the only package I was carrying. We stopped at a nice Chinese restaurant and suddenly the back of my mouth starts to water, my stomach tightens up, my eyes are bounce back and forth looking for a restroom. I get to the bathroom and no sooner than I open the door to the stall vomit is everywhere and my nostrils are flaming from where regurgitated soda passed through. I patted my face with cold water and returned to the table.

"Baby, do you feel alright?" Gbenga asked.

"Yes, but I'm pregnant." Just like that, I kept it real, wasted no time and studied his expression.

"Really? Really?" His face wore a smile, his eyes got brighter.

"Yes, I am and I know the timing is not great, but I think together we can work it out." He smiled and hugged me close. I can't believe the same arms that I desired so much would soon be the same ones to nearly rip me in two.

We talked and kissed and spent the rest of the day and night planning. Two days later a friend of his was having a party for his birthday. He wanted us to attend. We went to uptown Houston to the Galleria to go shopping. He pulled out a stack of money and told me I would need to buy a dress. I remember looking at many of the stores in the mall Emporio Armani, Gianni Versace, Chanel, Gucci, Dolce & Gabbana, Saks Fifth Avenue, Fendi, Barney's New York, I laughed to myself thinking: I recognize the names from fashion design classes, but Columbus didn't have any flagship designer stores. Gbenga looked at me and laughed. "Come on, I know where you'll find something you'll love."

We went inside Gianni Versace, and everyone knew his name. I have always had money to shop, and I had nice taste in clothes, but it does something to you to have ladies from a couture shop fighting over which one should help you. I was in there for an hour and ten minutes until I found the right dress. It was sweet, it fit like body paint against my skin, the silk added a swing at my waist, and right below my knee, the fabric just dripped like water. I picked out some black and gold stiletto mules from Gucci to go with the dress and I was ready for the party.

That evening as we pulled up to his friend Tunde's house, judging from the cars in the driveway, I was glad I had gone shopping. We got in the party and from the warm introductions I felt as though Gbenga must have told them about me. The women in Texas: well, the saying that Texans like 'em big stood out in my mind; big breasts, big hair, and big booties, wall to wall weavage and cleavage. Each one of these women had a different beauty from "ba-da-bing" to "bling, bling", each one of them stood out. Tunde walked over with a nice-looking girl on his arm, and introduced her as his girlfriend. She was going to the kitchen so I asked her if she needed any help. I followed her to bring out more drinks and a tray of shrimp. We had some small talk and then she asked me a question that made my ears ring. "So, how do you get along with the rest of Gbenga's children?"

I wanted to swallow my own tongue. Suddenly my one thousand eight hundred dollar Gianni Versace dress that made me feel like a diva divine turned into a bargain special from the Value City's circular. I couldn't utter a word. I did not want to give her the satisfaction of thinking she had something over on me. As I felt my hand reaching for something to hold onto, I looked her straight into her eyes, breathed in through my nose, and said, "Oh, yea, we get along great."

The room protracted at that moment, the blaring rhythm of the afro beat seemed to be tuned into the background. It was as if I had tunnel vision and all I could see was Gbenga standing in the corner clutching a beer, the flashes of his teeth as he looked my direction. I kept on smiling, afraid if I stopped I just might scream. I have never been the type of sista that fronted on her man in public. I had no intention of being disrespectful, but deep inside, my stomach was churning, and with every step the ground was loosening at my feet. At the moment our eyes met, I know he sensed something was different. I asked, "Hey baby, would you like to dance?"

"You know I really don't dance," he said, elevating his beer, as if to show me it was too much to leave unguarded.

So I took his hand up to my mouth and kissed it gently, then I pulled closely to his ear talking through my teeth in an endearing tone: "Either you are going to dance with me, or you are going to think of an excuse for why we are leaving." I backed up, still holding his hand and let him see my face, a delicate smile, mouth closed, lips just slightly upturned. Then I gave him a slow wink of my right eye. He clutched his arm around my back rocking with the music.

"Do you have a child already? Do you have children?" I looked to see his response, but I really didn't want to hear it.

"Who told you?" He snorted dismissively.

"Maybe you didn't hear me. I want to know if you have another child?"

"Yes." He said and gently pulled me closer to his chest. "I love you, I want to marry you."

"Why did I have to hear about this from someone else? Why would you let someone have the satisfaction of having something over me?" My face was puzzled, but I wasn't sure which hurt me worse- knowing that I wasn't giving him his first child, or the fact he kept something so important from me.

Then he said with that melodious voice, "You didn't hear me, I said I want to marry you."

Now we had talked about this before. He knew I admitted being unprotected was foolhardy, but I had expressed to him my feelings about having a child out of wedlock. But at that moment, coming from his mouth, that sweet shuffle of game became a one knee proposal.

We went to his place that night and made love like nothing I experienced before. Everything was slow and gentle. As soon as we hit the door he walked behind me with his hands on my waist and I could feel his manhood getting hard as a rock. My body was fluttering and urging. He gently kissed the back of my neck over and over softly with his lips using the slightest bit of tongue. He pressed me up against the closet door, pressing his chest into my back, and then he pulled up my dress, gathering up the silk until it met the small of my back. Then he dropped to his knees kissing the soft part on the back of my knees, trailing the curve of my thighs, his soft full lips brushing up and over my ass and gently finding a landing on the deft at the small of my back. My lips slightly parted, I exhaled a deep warm breath. He turned me around, pressing his mouth and chin into the soft fleshy part of my mound that lay beneath my thong. He ripped my thong and it fell like a ribbon, passed my ankles and onto the floor. He gently kissed and licked until he found my clit, rolling my nipple with the tips of his fingers. My whole body was on fire, every nerve was at attention, as he unzipped my dress and let it drop to the carpet at my feet. He lay me down and entered me slowly at first, adding pressure, as his chest wet with sweat came down on my nipples. His motions were rhythmic; I absorbed each sensation as he thrusted inside of me, a pleasurable pain. His eyes met with mine, then I felt my body overcome with ecstasy and I shuddered from my release.

That was probably one of the sweetest nights I remember. I say sweet because at that moment, after he came, when I lay in his arms, my head lowered on his shoulder, he looked at me full in my face and said he was sorry. It wasn't in the nonchalant way I have grown detached from. This was the only time I recall him saying with full conviction, what he was claiming responsibility for: "I am sorry for lying to you. I am sorry for not telling you I had children. I was scared to lose you." I held on to the tear-stained pillow. It should have told me a bit of who he was, the man who could make me moan with the sweetest taboo, the one who made me scream in passion and scream in pain.

As my stomach grew, so did my need for stability. Gbenga had asked me to turn down the offer to work in California. He knew clothing design had been a passion of mine for some time; it was only a back- up plan to get my degree in Marketing. At that time I saw his request as a step to be a unit, not an attempt to negate my worth. We were still living in different states. My catering jobs were going well, but I just got my degree and I wanted more. I picked up my business plan and headed downtown to the SBA office. When I came back, I got on the phone and called Gbenga. He sounded indifferent when I told him my plans; his voice was void, like someone talking on the phone when they'd rather be watching a ball game. I hung up the phone and several questions kept bouncing in my head. I went to the edge of my bed and prayed that night; "God show me a sign from somewhere that this is meant to be."

3
Spiral Bound

I got off in London, and the terminal seemed surreal. I had been there so many times before either to West Africa or from West Africa, but this time was different. I had no desires to shop duty free, to eat, or buy a t-shirt showing where I had been. The only longing I had was that my children were with me. My arms felt so lifeless, as usually I would be loaded down with one child in my arms and another one close behind ready to dart towards any toy store he saw. I hadn't eaten anything for more than ten hours, but the pain in my heart far outweighed the one in my stomach. The far off look in my oldest son's face preoccupied my mind. His expression as he packed his suitcase searching around his room deciding what to take was branded in my memory. I can't remember exactly when he stopped expressing, his eyes becoming void of the childish sparkle and turning hazed, expectant. It was like he was always waiting for something to happen, but never surprised when it did. Like the build- up of the wave breaking against the beach near our house, he just kept quiet knowing it would happen as it did time and time again. No matter how big it got when it crested, he knew wherever it landed some of the sand would surely be sucked away from its path. I realized we robbed him, his father for abusing me, and me for accepting it.

I sat on a chair at the terminal noticing all of the gates, so many of them gateways to exotic places, foreign lands, but the one that caught my attention was the one I just passed through, back to my babies. I got on the phone to call a girlfriend. She helped me go to the U.S. Embassy the day before, she had suspicions I was leaving but I told her if I did I would call when I was safe.

"Hello?"

"Hi Sissy, it's Kim, I'm in London."

"Girl, are you sure, your husband has been calling all over everywhere wanting to know who you were staying with and did any of us know you were leaving. Are you o.k.?" I could hear a collective gasp of relief.

I could no longer hold it in. "Sissy, he has the boys, we got to the airport and he has the boys, I don't know…" With each tear, my breath drew shorter.

"Please, stop crying, stop crying. Do you want me to go check on them?"

"Yes, please." I wasn't sure if it would be possible, but I knew if anyone could get through the door Sissy could. I looked at her as a big sister. Flawless cocoa brown skin, the most welcoming spirit, and feistiness she brought from growing up on the South Side of Chicago. Her husband was a powerful man from Delta State, a shipping tycoon and president of a large petroleum company. He had the ear of the Vice President of Nigeria, but Sissy had his ear, and in their house, she was the Commander In Chief. Gbenga admired her husband and he wouldn't want to offend her.

Another voice came on the phone. Apparently, my frantic husband, searching to know who helped me to leave had awakened some of my girlfriends in the middle of the night. Which one of them knew I was trying to take HIS children out of the country? That possessive pronoun-his. Everything was his, the children, the cars, me, my thoughts, every minute of my day. I know how they must have felt. Gbenga had a way of convincing you that the answer you were giving him was somehow not the right one, or at least not the one he was looking to hear. His voice is like a strange melody, sweet blues dipping into your soul coveting your happiness and covering it with dark, slow tones.

"Hi Kim, it's Megan, Gbenga called all of us, so we all decided to come here and find out what was going on. Are you all right? Why didn't you tell us what was going on?"

"He has the boys. I am in London. He took them, and he told me Heather's husband called him to warn him I was leaving." My voice was falling all over itself with sadness.

The phone got quiet. Apparently Heather was there at the house with the "Wives", and they now had their answer to how my husband found out I was leaving. A fragile voice came on the telephone.

"I am really so sorry. I was hoping that my husband would talk to Gbenga and convince him to change his ways."

My nose was filled with snot, making it so hard for me to breathe. I fumbled through my purse looking for a tissue. I blew my nose and talked as fast as I could, aware the calling card could cut off any minute. "Do you have any idea what you've done? Did you think I was leaving simply because I was sick of the place? Do you know what danger you could have put me in Heather? He was kicking my ass! It was not a lover's quarrel, he was kicking my ass! Two of my ribs are cracked, my ear was bleeding, and he burnt the back of my neck with a cigarette! What were you thinking?" I knew she clearly was not thinking. Heather's husband adored her. He spent most of his time pulling Nigeria onto the information age of the information highway, and what time he had left gently nudging his wife to embrace their new lifestyle.

"I'm sorry, I didn't know and I didn't think my husband would tell him. He told me he wouldn't tell him."

"Oh my God, Heather, how many of our husbands would let us leave with our children permanently? Regardless of any circumstance, he knew it wasn't a vacation. Ask Megan, she is getting pressure in her marriage just because she doesn't have any male children yet. Oh Heather, what did you do?"

I couldn't say another word, my mind could no longer think, I gave them the number to my grandparents' house and hung up the receiver.

My grandfather was the next person I called. He and I had a strained relationship since my grandmother died some months before, but they always said if things got bad the boys and I had a place to stay. The inside of my head had a low hum to it, and I could feel the knot on my head was harder and the hair follicles seemed to systematically move with my heartbeat.

"Hello."

"Hello, Grandpa, it's me,"

"Hi Love Bugs, are you o.k? I got a call from a Mrs. Barker at the U.S Embassy in Nigeria. She told me that you would be calling. How are the boys?"

"The boys are not with me. He wouldn't let me take them. I am in London."

"The boys aren't with you? Why did you leave them? What about the Embassy? They told me that they were helping you leave. They told me how you came into the consulate with your face bruised and that. . The boys aren't with you?" His voice was dripping with disbelief.

"No, Grandpa, he came to the airport with some immigration officers and..."

"Well, I guess you will have to go back. I am going to call the lady from the State Department. I have her number." His voice trailed off. I couldn't even believe my ears. How was I going to go back? If I were dead, would that help my children? How I yearned for my grandmother to be on the other end of that phone. She knew my heart. She would never question my love for my boys. My mind trailed off. I put the receiver down and rested my head on the cold steel of the telephone booth. Standing there, bowed over with my head in my hands at the phone stand, flash backs and old conversations came flooding through my mind.

*****

The first time he hit me I was pregnant, in my fifth month, but barely showing. I wore baggy clothes and warm-up gear. I was in Texas for a visit celebrating my grant certificate from the city of Columbus to open a restaurant. Gbenga and I were happy and discussing the concept and interior of what the place would look like. I had already acquired a property that I could rent per month. It had formally been a strip club, but the grant money was really given to help improve the district with newer, more community-friendly businesses. Doors seemed to be opening, for Gbenga too. He had been working in communications at local television stations since he had left Texas Southern University. He always wanted to get into promotions and entertainment after working weekends spent with his cousin's band lining up shows and working as a soundman. Just one week prior, he was able to book one of the largest Reggae entertainers in the industry to perform at a show he was promoting at a local park. My heart was abloom with promise and excitement of the things to come for us. We just came back to his place after walking the dogs. He went upstairs to take a shower. All of a sudden his cell phone and his pager went off. I answered his cell phone. "Click"

I picked up the cell phone and the pager and carried both of them to the bathroom. The pager went off again.

"69 911"

Suddenly I became suspicious; Sixty-Nine is a code synonymous for booty calls from the opposite sex. The phone rang again. I picked it up. "Hello."

All I heard was quiet breathing and a woman's voice in the background. "Click." I got to the bathroom, opened the door and put his phone and pager on the granite counter top.

"Your phone was ringing and your pager is going off crazy."

"Who was it?"

"I don't know, they hung up on me, twice."

The water from the shower stopped. I heard the shower door come open but I turned to walk down the steps. Ten minutes later Gbenga emerges from the bedroom wearing jeans and a Bob Marley t-shirt.

"I'll be right back. I need to buy some cigarettes," he said. Normally it wouldn't have struck me as anything, but I observed his posture as he was talking, very rushed and agitated.

Now the store is at the corner, a ten minute walk, but he left in the car. Twenty five minutes later, he spins into the driveway, cigarette resting in his mouth. He gets out of the car, comes in the house and starts rumbling in the cabinets.

"Baby, are you looking for something?" I said confused by his demeanor. He didn't answer, but I could hear his pager vibrating in his pants pocket. "Gbenga, your pager is going off. Someone must really need to talk to you urgently," I said with a tint of sarcasm in my voice. His face became overcast with clouds of darkness, and then all of a sudden, in one swift motion my mouth met with his backhand. I felt the soft flesh inside my bottom lip open, tasting blood and saliva.

"Did anyone ask you to pick up my phone? Why is your mouth so smart?" he said in a low dark voice, lines on his forehead starting to appear.

I couldn't say a word, my eyes were watering, but I wasn't about to cry, I was stunned. I touched my lip, starting to feel it swell. I looked up at him from the corner of my eye, lowered my eyelids and turned to walk away.

"I am sorry, baby, I don't know what happened," he said apologetically, as though the slap from his backhand was a muscle spasm.

I packed my bags that day too, to leave and go home, but I stayed. That was the day I began to turn against myself, to question, not about leaving him, but about what I could have done to change what he did. I was partially at fault. Why did I get sassy? Even though he had told me to answer his phone several times before, maybe I shouldn't have picked it up. I was having his baby. If we were going to be a family, wouldn't that make him the head of the house? I started to feel bad that I was questioning him.

Staples

"Virgin Air Flight 143 is now boarding out of Gate C36," a welcoming voice called over the airport address system. My back straightened out, I could feel the pains in my sides, bruises wrapped like a tight corset along my sides. I could hear the blaring of the receiver dangling from its cord at the phone stand. I removed the ticket jacket from my pocket, I noticed the luggage claim tickets stapled on the jacket that were not my own. I was going to make this journey by myself.

*****

Naming children at birth are the first pronouncements of love for your children. Sometimes they are given as predictions and affirmations. We named our sons after strong Black revolutionaries; Steven Biko, a South African who fought against Apartheid, and Malcolm X, "by any means necessary". Both were men of strength and purpose, leaders. Ironically, after the years of excuses and explanations to my children about what was happening when daddy was arguing with me behind the locked door, or how I had an accident, the fact that I gave them such strong names almost began to mock me. At night I would tuck them in with stories of brave men who stood up against numbers of people to do what they believed was right; I would kiss them on their foreheads and cower before a man who was oppressing my very existence. Every revolution has bloodshed, casualties. It wasn't fear of my blood being shed that gripped me night after night, scared to change the channel on the television because it might set him off. It was the fear that my boys might become the casualties. I had long grown tired of Malcolm standing in as a referee during some of our arguments. He would be playing with his toys or watching cartoons when I noticed he would straighten up all of the sudden, drop his eyelids and cock his head. It was like a well- trained dog that heard sounds that other people could not hear. Then Malcolm would spring up from wherever he was, go to the door and give his father a bear hug. It didn't happen all of the time, but after a while I noticed it happened whenever Gbenga's footsteps were slightly heavier against the marble floor, or if the sound the door made when it closed echoed louder against its wooden frame than usual. It was as though he was gauging his daddy's temperature by his movements and felt his hugs would become a coolant for his aggression. Sometimes he would be in his room when the fights started, and I would see a small shadow in the crack of the doorway. Then, I would walk into another room, aware I would be followed by my husband, but at least the fighting would not be in front of him. There were so many secrets we would hide. I became very good at making excuses and hiding bruises, which became a paradox. I would come up with excuses and stories to save him from embarrassment and ridicule; I became very convincing. But Gbenga was only convinced it made me a good liar, and as a liar I should be watched closely.

*****

My restaurant opened and was doing very well. One of my older brothers helped me gut the place and do all of the remodeling inside. Local and small neighborhood newspapers were writing articles about "the piece of Jamaica in the heart of the Short North." Sweets and spices lured workers in from their offices for an Island break and the dinner crowd enjoyed well- dressed plates of West Indian paradise. We had a great location, between the OSU campus and downtown. The flavor was Caribbean and the sounds were Reggae. Business was going well. The people came in faster than I could cook. I wanted to hire a native Jamaican cook and some more staff, but money was really tight. Malcolm was still breastfeeding and my breasts were engorged. I was due to take some time off to wean him to the bottle. I called Gbenga and he said he would come up to manage the restaurant and talk to a friend of his about getting a cook from Jamaica. A few days later he arrived at the restaurant with a young man carrying his bags. He introduced me to Peter, the guy who was going to be the new cook. I talked to Peter, who stood very alert, thin body and dangling fingers with eyes full of curiosity. I showed him around the kitchen and discussed the dishes we offered on the menu. He sat very quietly without saying a word, teeth flashing in the sunlight that peered through the front windows.

"Where did you find him at? Did you just take him off the boat? I asked Gbenga, only half kidding.

"You remember the Caribbean restaurant on Westheimer? Yea, well, he just came in from Jamaica, Mandeville, his papers aren't clean, but I will pay him myself until you can manage to get things in order. I also think you should hire two more wait staff."

He reached inside of his bag and brought out a stack of money and gave it to me. I don't know what made me think first, the nonchalant way he handed me the money or the fact each stack was separated with rubber bands. I asked Peter to show me what he could cook. I was eating for two. I wanted to know how well he could cook and I needed an opportunity to talk to Gbenga while the traffic in the restaurant was slow. I never thought I was naive, and I knew Columbus was a small town, but that day small pieces of a puzzle that were my man's life were coming together. I looked at the faces of the bills and saw that they were all twenty dollar bills, four inches high, wrapped with two rubber bands, sitting on the table! I asked him where the money came from, but before he could say a word I believed I knew the answer.

"It's better you don't know," he said, resting back in the chair and bringing out a cigarette.

"No, I think it's better I do. The pagers, the cell phones, picking you up at different people's houses every time you come to visit me, are routine, but that doesn't make it normal. We are having a baby. I really need to know!" My voice cracked and my eyes opened wide.

We stayed up all night talking. I asked a lot of questions I should have asked more than a year ago. In simplest terms, Gbenga was a baller. He had been dealing drugs through most of our relationship, and in Columbus of all places.

*****

While in college I saw some ballers at the campus parties, posted up at the back of the party with their ball caps on and their Karl Kani gear, or their team jerseys. It was like a hip-hop carnival, bright colors and loud jewelry. I had a few girlfriends who would stay out late after the party was over to hang in the parking lot gawkin' at the pimped-out cars, painted candy colors with the custom-made sound systems that made the pavement jump as they rode by. But I never saw Gbenga like that. He had a regal disposition, was very well dressed and had shoes that always shined like money. He was quiet, but his posture commanded attention. When he moved, the atmosphere seemed to move with him. He was engaging, with invisible boundaries; most people didn't move within six feet of him. I was aware he had money, but he was not flashy. I often asked him questions, but they were evaded. He needed money; he had a lot of responsibilities.

I always admired him for the way he was able to put his siblings through college and take care of his children, but it never occurred to me the kind of money he was spending or to question where it was coming from. I was in love with him.

*****

After he fell off to sleep, I picked Malcolm up from his crib and lay skin to skin with his curl- covered head resting calmly on my chest, I rubbed gently on his back, his blue velour onesy crushing beneath my fingers. I sang softly and lowered my eyes as I looked over at Gbenga sleeping. What I learned that night I did not want for Gbenga, I did not want it for me or the baby. Gbenga asked me to hold on, he would soon be out of the game. He just needed a little time and a little more money. I felt there was nothing for me to do but relax and accept that he knew what he was doing.

This visit was longer than most of the visits we shared. I had asked Gbenga to come into the restaurant so we could spend some more time together. He would sit there in the back of the restaurant, like a mama bird very observant of her nest, reading the paper. Occasionally one or two people would come in to talk to him, his smiles fleeting, slow and informed, keeping most people off balance. It was obvious to me from Gbenga's posture, relaxed back in the chair, one elbow resting on the armrest, head cocked down and eyes roving over each bag or crease in each jacket, that these people were business associates and not friends coming to talk old times.

Our relationship was steady for a year or two after that. I discovered when money is good, a man's sex drive is off the chain. During the day I was the owner of a growing restaurant. Gbenga had bought a brand new state of the art Bang & Olufsen sound system for the restaurant and replaced the once used chairs which I had upholstered myself with new mahogany chairs from Italy, with soft straight leather backs. But in the late evenings I would entertain a different crowd of guests at our house. For some time I convinced myself I had stability, an immaculate four bedroom split-level house, a man, a beautiful baby boy and a thriving business. Gbenga's business started booming too. What started out as something that would keep him busy for a couple of hours, on the phones, spilled over into a warehousing business. Maybe I could have said more. After all I saw how few Black men I started college with actually made it through to graduation. Not enough money to go to school, not enough jobs to go around. I knew the problems a Black brotha faces day to day. We stayed up many times talking about it. I toiled with myself over and over about the moralities and legalities, user and dealers, drugs tearing up families. I even watched Gbenga sometimes, slumped over in a chair, eyebrows furrowing, going on about whether or not he furthered the Black man's problem by supplying poison that was ending up on the streets. I questioned and I sympathized; my heart was tearing and his was becoming harder. I wanted to support my man, in whatever his endeavors were. But now I was running a restaurant by day, and running a transport service to and from the airport between Texas and Columbus, picking up dope runners and dropping them off at hotels. Each day I mixed myself a blind girl's cocktail: part naivete, part love, and a jigger of ignorance. Slowly a cool burn was developing in my throat from each gulp. The mules were often guys, and occasionally very pretty girls. They realized I was Gbenga's girl, and would show up at the restaurant the next day, sit down, cool as you please, and eat lunch. They would sit at the table with the air of a poser, dressed right, but actin' wrong. Some of them would talk loud and clap their hands for the waitress, "showing their ass". Gbenga and I needed to talk.

Gbenga always called me a communist; he said I didn't like money. He claimed my frugality was one of the things that attracted him to me. The truth was we both liked money for what it could help us do for the people we love, but I was just more practical in my spending. He saw a Range, I saw a Jeep. He saw a $7,000 Cartier bangle, I saw a tennis bracelet. He saw a $2,500 dress from Dolce and Gabanna, I just saw an overblown little black dress. I was just more efficient with money, that's all. I liked fine things, but at what price was I willing to pay to get them? My restaurant was growing into a success and gaining good reviews in the local papers. We had a gift in a beautiful child, and I felt I had shown my loyalty and faith in us. I saw nothing wrong with him leaving the hustle and helping me expand the restaurant. He knew several people in the music industry; we could have live shows on weekends. We could get a liquor license. I believed we could make it work with what we had. Gbenga sat down in front of me, his eyes lowered and shoulders back.

"No matter how big you talk, how strong you are, you are not a man. You are just starting, we have a baby, I need the chance to take care of my family and be in charge of myself. Do you want to stop me before I have had a chance to do that?" he asked.

I sat and pondered on his comment. All I ever wanted to do was have a man who made his own way and be his woman at home building him up. I wanted to create a beautiful home, a place where there was peace to make my man happy. But what peace is there when it risked losing the very man I was trying to protect? The two possibilities had no appeal to me; loss by incarceration or gangland style death both left a bitter taste of saliva in my mouth.

*****

I boarded the flight to the United States from London, my heart still heavy, my tears washed away leaving caramel-colored lame' streaks down my face. I walked the aisles of the plane in a deep haze only lifting my eyelids to see the numbers above the seats. I put my hands in my purse to retrieve my boarding pass, my fingers stretching. I felt something smooth, cold, and almost plastic-like. I reached further into my bag and pulled out a small action figure that I had packed for my youngest son. Immediately the inside of my nose started to tingle and tears filled up my eyes. I sat down in the first empty seat I had come to, gazing at this tiny action figure as if I had a piece of heaven in my palm.

Push Pin

"Kimmy! Kimmy!" Gbenga called out. That sweet melodious African accent had now turned raspy and sour. Somewhere during our relationship I stopped being a partner and realized I had become a soldier-some days a street soldier, but most days just ready to drop anything I was doing to stand at attention.

"Yea, baby, hold on," I responded back in a loud whisper as I trailed down the steps. "I was just putting the boys to sleep."

"What kind of shit is this?" he asked, eyes wide and face full of fury holding the cover to a pot that was on the stove.

"It's spaghetti. There is some sauce in the oven. I made it with meatballs," I replied, opening the oven door and trying to stretch to leave the least possible space between us.

"I haven't eaten all day and you expect me to eat this shit? Why would I come back to Africa and eat this? You just feed me anything…" His voice

The Links

My third month in Nigeria and I met an older African-American woman, Mrs. Fafiati at the grand opening of a children's activity center in Lagos. She was thin and frail and wore her hair in a bob. I could tell she was at least in her sixties, but her smile and bright eyes were so alive and youthful. She immediately extended her hand to mine and brought in her shoulders as though she was going to greet me with a kiss, but instead gave a closed mouth smile and grasped my hand with her other hand resting on top of mine. She was from Connecticut and was very warm and witty. She too was also married to a Nigerian man, but he was now deceased. I found it amazing that at her age she remained in Nigeria and seemed to have adjusted very well. We made small talk, laughed and joked for about an hour. We exchanged telephone numbers and addresses, and she reached into a beautifully woven raffia bag and handed me a piece of paper. It was a newsletter of some sort for the American Women's Association. I loaded the boys in the back of the jeep and drove home with a huge smile. I went to my brother in-law's house where we were staying for the moment and talked to Gbenga about my afternoon. I am sure he saw the cheeriness in my voice and the joy that had spread throughout my body. I so loved Nigeria, but now I had the opportunity of discussing experiences with a fellow American. I handed him the newsletter and asked him if it would be all right for me to attend the meeting. He quietly shrugged his shoulders and said he would try to locate the directions so I could drive myself.

They were mainly wives of oil workers; most were dainty white women and a sprinkling of African- American women who filled the room. The meeting was held at an American Embassy clubhouse. It seemed so far from Nigeria with its American menu and baroque upholstery. Only the tropical ginger floral arrangements and a few sparse pieces of artwork had a Nigerian flare. There were tiny finger foods, American delights that I had not seen since I left home; brownies, cucumber finger sandwiches, cheese balls with Ritz crackers, and mini hot-dogs, all arranged in beautifully adorned china trays. Ladies drank coffee, talked, and showed off the latest things they had bought from the local markets. The meeting started mid-morning where they discussed upcoming events, charitable fundraisers, and community service initiatives. This gathering was nearing its end when the organization's president called for any new people to stand and introduce themselves. I stood up, introduced myself, told what brought me to Nigeria and how long I had been there. As the meeting finished many ladies welcomed me, but I knew right away that my connection was strongest with the WIVES.

On Saturday I picked up Mrs. Fafiati and she accompanied my boys and me to what would be my first meeting with the Wives. We walked into the meeting room, which had been an elementary classroom just the day before, and took our seats. Attendance seemed to be small, but a very diverse gathering of many cultures was represented in that room. I recognized a few faces from the American Women's meeting, but these faces were slightly older and more attentive. Women from many countries graced that room, and what would simply be looked at as Black and White, as far as one's pigment, now were beautiful shades of the rainbow, each one brought together by the love for their Nigerian husbands. I observed the gestures each would give the other and was tickled by the different accents that wafted through the room. With the ring of a bell, a tall, beautifully brown, well-built West Indian lady stood at the front of the room. All of the ladies backed away and found their seats.

"Welcome. Can we please have all guests stand?" she asked, gesturing her hands like she was directing a choir.

Right away Mrs. Fafiati nudged my shoulder and winked for me to stand up and introduce myself.

"Good afternoon, my name is Kim, I recently moved to Lagos from Ohio." Encouraged by the smiles and handshakes, I nodded and quickly took my seat. The meeting continued with talks of the large fundraiser and an upcoming bar-be-que with the husbands. Then an older lady, a White woman dressed in Nigerian dress who spoke with a crisp British accent, stood up and read an invitation to all of the Wives who would like to attend an upcoming wedding. Suddenly voices rose, like birds that had just been startled into flight. I looked at Mrs. Fafiati in bewilderment.

"This is what we do. From now on, we are your family and we represent you at all occasions where you may need a family to stand in for you," she explained, her warm smile returning. It was also tradition for friends of the mother to attend the wedding wearing dresses all cut from the same fabric-aso ebi, if you were Yoruba. All of the women gathered to order fabric so they could have the cloth sewn in their own unique style in time for the wedding. Suddenly I felt at ease realizing that the noise was glorious approval and support, for yet another babe was leaving the nest.

I would attend many meetings after that. I felt so passionate about the work they did locally with the Braille Centre and the many issues that affected us as wives: land ownership, voting, and alien status. Africa is a continent full of erroneous issues regarding gender: female circumcision, bigamy, status, widowhood rights, stoning, the list goes on. But what was hard for me to swallow was the issue of giving up one's country and possibly even your family for the love of a man. You were not entitled to anything which you helped that man build. The mere notion of it was like hot palm oil being poured into my ears.

Ninety- eight percent of the women in the Wives club loved

Nigeria. I was among those women. I loved the colors of the people, the friendly smiles and fragile curiosity that greeted you, the beautiful angelic faces of the children when they played soccer on the beach, and the sweet and sour smell of over-ripe mangoes that fell from the trees in the villages as they baked in the sun. Oh, and the beach, white sand and towering waves that broke into a million tiny bubbles against the water's edge. I felt the country was so underutilized as a tourist attraction and a few military rogues ruined it for many people who were respectful, intelligent and hard- working. Then there was the minority within the Wives: two percent that saw Nigeria for everything it wasn't. They hated everything from the epileptic electric supply to the fact they could not buy Oreos at the local supermarket. They bickered about their husbands and their in-laws, and couldn't understand why, if their husband loved them, why he would want to see them live in squalor. These women were typically the fledgling ones, the neophytes, as was I, so I saw it a challenge to bring them to the meetings and redirect their focus from half empty to half full. I really enjoyed the Wives as a collective. I never did hang out in a posse of girls growing up. But the Wives had a mission, a constitution, an order. They just needed some fresh perspective. There were many who had carried the torch and paved the way into great services for the communities in which they lived. My thoughts and youthfulness seemed to be a fresh set of legs for the continued journey.

I breathed new life into some old events and planned fresh ones, none of which my husband would ever attend. What I did enjoy was the ease in which these "sisters" and I could talk. The confidence they seemed to have in me, I needed that contentment. It contradicted the eggshells I was walking on at home, the times I made myself so small and Gbenga so big. What developed during these exchanges kept the floor beneath my feet and kept me from melting further and faster into the floor with each teardrop. There was an increased attendance and an admiration filled the air among members. I knew, however, that only a small percent of it was for me, because I was simply an ignition to the flame that burnt so bright in each one of them.

I loved the Wives. I learned things from them that I would have been too embarrassed or ashamed to ask my in-laws, who had changed dramatically since my arrival into Nigeria as my home, and no longer the place I just visited. Gbenga never liked any one of these friendships. Mind you, some of these women were older than me, some much older, wiser, more cultured, and educated, had time-tested and stronger marriages, but he never wanted any of them too close. They were either too chatty, too bourgeois, and my favorite among all that he accused was that one of them "wanted to use my youth to pull in contracts from Nigerian businessmen". So in other words, he said I was being "pimped."

Safety Pin

The plane landed in the States and I went directly to the customs desk. I had to surrender my passport until I was able to pay the money back to the U.S. Embassy which was used to fly me out of Nigeria. I was relieved that the chaperone of my passport said there would be careful consideration time before I returned, and saddened at the thought of my children possibly needing me, but the money would serve as a weight bearing on my return. My stomach felt empty and my head was light. My first journey without my children, I had no idea how I was going to hold on. My bags were quickly inspected by the U.S. customs officials; I had nothing to declare, no African foods, none of the usual art work I would bring home as gifts to family members, and my most precious gifts were thousands of miles away across many bodies of water and billions of grains of sand. I picked up my luggage and headed towards the passenger pick up. The sun pushed through the concrete corridor of the airport terminal. The air was stale, no more savory scents or harmattan dust in the air. I turned, gazing at all of the cars lined up like participants in a parade, passengers putting luggage in the trunk, receiving hugs and kisses from family members and excited faces. Tears of joy were streaming down blissful faces and words of welcome reverberated against the sound of airplanes overhead. Loneliness built up inside me, my hands clutching my luggage and my head spinning from the last twenty-four hours. I realized my grandfather had not changed his mind. I went to the pay phone and called my cousin.

"Hey Stacy, it's Kimmy, I am at Port Columbus and I need a place to stay. Can I come by?"

Her scream on the other end of the phone gave me a temporary solace; I had a place to stay.

My first night was difficult. My tears were unmanageable and I called out to my boys. I sobbed until I fell down to my knees, carpet wet with tears and snot, as I prayed to God to watch over my boys and help me make it through these next couple of days.

I have always had a difficult time accepting charity, and I needed a distraction, so immediately I knew it was time for me to get a job. Each day that passed I would look at the want ads or fill out applications, until my fingers were stained with newsprint. I yearned for an interview, but wasn't sure the hole in my heart could be concealed with enough needed enthusiasm to pull me through. I longed to hear from my grandmother, whose peaceful tone and virtuous spirituality helped me through some of my worst times. I missed her soft toasted almond complexion, her face, aged and wise, and her big beautiful brown eyes that she lined in Fashion Fair brown. She always said so much without saying much at all. "Baby, let God do His work," she would say, or "This is all just preparation for the great thing God is getting ready to do in your life."

In my heart I knew she was telling the truth, but if God knew the ending, I just wanted to see the trailer of the next couple of scenes, so I knew which way to go.

I received a message that morning that my grandfather was trying to reach me. I walked to the kitchen and picked up the phone.

"Hello," he answered softly.

"Hello, Grandpa, it's Kimmy, I was told you were trying to reach me."

His voice picked up. "Hi, Love Bugs, Gbenga has been calling here asking of you. Do you want me to give him a number to reach you?"

"Yea, that's fine, did you talk with the boys?" I said, my voice cracking as I pulled a chair close to sit down.

"I talked with them. They miss you, maybe you should…" He talked, but I pulled the phone away from my ear.

"Go back and risk worse because I dared to try and take my children with me?," The tone in my voice was getting higher. "Did you ask him what he did to me, how he did it in front of the boys?"

"Yes, he said he hit you, but he also said there was no way he would let you take Malcom and Steven, so you have to go back to those babies."

"Thank you for the message. You can give him Stacy's number. I'll talk with you later." I hung up the phone. This time it wasn't sadness I felt, but a cool chill that blew into my ear and down against my spine. Gbenga's goal was not to keep the boys, but to keep control of me. I decided to call the house in Nigeria. I looked at the clock, and figured by this time the boys should be home from school.

"Yeah," Gbenga answered the phone.

My lips parted but my words were stuck in my throat. "Hi, Gbeng, my Grandfather said you wanted to talk with me. How are the boys?"

"The boys are good. Are you in Ohio?"

"Yes, I am staying with my cousin." It was like hypnosis, as soon as I heard his voice I recoiled like a child giving explanations of my movements.

"I wanted to make sure you were there before I let them go back to school," he replied. The response took me off guard. Why wouldn't they be in school? Was he trying to move them away so I wouldn't see them again?

"Out of school?" I asked through gritted teeth. "Why wouldn't they be in school?"

"I didn't want you or any of your friends taking them from me. You wanted to sneak them off." His voice was stoic and harsh, "I thought you were at the U.S. embassy all of this time, just waiting for your opportunity to kidnap them."

My face was riddled with astonishment. "Gbenga, I tried reasoning with you, separate bedrooms, separation, I was even willing to go to the village to stay with my in-laws until we got counseling, I was just tired of the hitting and what it was doing to the children." Strangely, the release of the words drew my attention to my feet. I did not feel the usual slipping feeling that always caused me to watch my words.

"I don't know what happened. I shouldn't have been hitting you. It's just that I am under enormous pressure here. I have a state of the art filling station and road pirates prevent me from keeping gas in it. Nigeria is stressful, business is stressful, you are the closest one to me, and so you get the worst of it. I'm sorry." As soon as he said the words there was a dead silence on the line. The hum and the static that usually accompanies all international trunks was undetectable. All I could hear was the inhale of my own breath as I filled up my lungs with streams of courage that would get me through this call.

"I know about the pressure. I felt it too. Did you think it was easy for me fetching water, periods of time with no light, not being able to talk to family or friends for months, being ostracized by members of your family, malaria, washing loads of clothes by hand, no light, no diesel to run the generator, boiling water for the boys to have a warm bath, feeling like an alien. Did you think I always enjoyed it? I was doing it for you, for us. You wanted to go back to your country and contribute to the new democracy, and I wanted to follow you. I felt everything you felt and I tried to help. When money was tight I sold the Land Rover, MY CAR. Now I am here with nothing to drive and you have a choice of four luxury cars in your driveway. Would I do that if I wasn't trying to love you, to help you? We weren't the first to come back to Nigeria. I am sure everyone has growing pains. I could take the culture change, even the inconveniences, but I did not deserve the abuse." I let out my breath, but I didn't hear a response.

"Mom?" The small voice tickled my ears and tugged at my heart.

"Yes, baby it's me. How are you? Mommy misses you so much," I said, words rolling out of my tight smile. "How about the dollar, do you still have it?" thinking of our last parting moments brought tears slowly down my face.

"Yea, Mommy, I have it. Where are you? Will you come back?" Malcolm questioned.

"I know you are taking care of your brother, aren't you? Is he there with you?"

Steven came to the phone. His energy moved through the phone line. "Hey Mom!"

"Hey Steven, I love you."

"I know, Mom, I love you. When ya coming back, Mommy?" Steven's words were short and brief but the impact on my heart was just as meaningful had he talked for hours. I knew I was missing so much just from not being there with them. The moments would be gone forever, lost in time. I couldn't hear anything else, but I sensed Malcolm's presence over the phone. I used to stand beside his bed while he was sleeping just finding joy in hearing him breathe and watching his tiny chest move up and down.

"Malcolm baby? You know I love you, Malcolm?" I called out to him.

"Yeah, I know. I miss you, Mom," he paused. "I talked to Daddy and he promised me if you came back he wouldn't do it again, Mom." His words spoke with confident assurance like a young man, I wasn't sure he was convinced himself of what he said.

"Well, baby, I would like nothing more than to be with you, but I can't right now." Too soon the voice prompt from the calling card system could be heard on the phone, there was one minute of time left.

"Malcolm, the phone is getting ready to cut, I want you to know I love you. Tell your brother I love him so much. I want nothing more than to hold you in my arms. Be a good boy, do well in school, and I will"- the phone line went dead. My words weren't enough. I wondered if he could feel my love for him? I sat in that spot with the same blank stare long after the sun disappeared from the sky. I thought of every movement, every funny expression the boys had made since we had moved. Malcolm's bright eyes and slender frame, Steven's handsome lips, shaped like a perfect brown bow. The sounds of their voices danced around my head until I fell off to sleep.

Cruise control, I think it's a feature a man uses on his car, but a self-inflicted mode perfected by women. It's the pace you move when you are not sure of your purpose, but you keep on moving, because if you dare stop to think about what's going on you could lose your mind, your courage to push further, or maybe lose your life. I was crying myself to sleep, dosing off in the middle of prayers, reliving the separation of me and the boys in nightmares or welcoming them home in my dreams, only to wake up exhausted. Mornings were spent over the newspaper classifieds and a cup of juice. Some days I would catch the bus to a temporary employment agency or a mall, where I could fill out multiple applications. The cancerous cell of despair was multiplying at an alarming rate inside my body. Words from family members did not console me. My husband only attended one family function in over ten years of marriage, so no one would have anything to say in support of him because they didn't know him. There were also a couple of family members whose support was overlooked due to their overshadowing ignorance. "You shouldn't have gone to Africa in the first place. I could have told you he was going to get you over there and mistreat you, make you walk three feet behind him and cover your head. Most of them over there got at least three wives." They would talk back and forth at each other, more than they were talking to me. Pride was never an issue when I dealt with these relatives. I was not concerned about "I told you so" from any of them. They still thought Nigeria was like every National Geographic and Discovery Channel special they ever saw about Africa. They thought I was either over there bare-breasted foraging for berries and dodging lions or covered from head to toe in Muslim tradition, just happy to have the opportunity to speak when spoken to. Other members of my family could only tell me to hold on, that I would soon see my boys again. Most of them were not in a position to tell me what I was holding on to. They felt church was full of hypocrites, and I wasn't sure where their faith was, and mine was tested. The way I kept laying things down at the altar and picking them back up, the ushers lost direction, so I was holding onto "somewhere."

Masking Tape

You would think after my own experience of being adopted I would understand a child's bond with its mother, but every day the weight grew heavier. Girlfriends would call from Nigeria, "I had no idea, why didn't you come to me?" My life epitomized the term pretty mess; I had been acting to my friends. I had counseled many wives on domestic issues and kept my own hidden. I was humiliated by the hitting. The outside appearance of the beautiful home I shared with my husband, the well entertained parties, and all of it was a theatrical show, smoke and mirrors. The real Kim was not the one they saw at the meetings, balancing dutiful African wife, organized, resourceful businesswoman and doting mother, all with poise and control. I was a shell of myself, like the dozens washed on the shore of Eko Beach each day.

It had been three months in my job search and I was getting used to the jargon many employers use. I was riding buses and catching rides to many interviews only to be told I was over-qualified, or, with my skills I would probably not be willing to stay with the company for a long period of time. I just wanted a chance, an opportunity. The walls at my cousin's house were closing in on me; the laughs from her children only made me long for my own children more. No children, no money, no job, marriage failed, coulda, woulda, shoulda, all trampled through my head like children playing tag. "Why did I" constantly filled my head.

*****

The sun met me at my restaurant one morning. Malcolm was in his walker trying to maneuver to the tile floor, rather than the carpet where his little legs could pick up speed. I was mopping the floor, changing dinner menus to lunch menus and checking stock. As the sun was breaking through the blinds in the windows I noticed a stockily built man standing on the sidewalk. I walked closer to the window to look. He was staring straight at me, square white face and blank stare. I had a visit from the Health Inspector nearly a week before with no citations, so I knew he could not be from their office. But he kept standing there, which struck me as peculiar because at that time of the morning on High Street most people would be going to work, and even the homeless would have staggered onto the food kitchen line. I wrapped the last set of cutlery in the napkin and placed it on the table. I gathered my baby and the diaper bag and moved towards the door. When I opened the door, the lunch crowd was boppin', the sweet scent of coco bread and beef patties filled the air. Bob Marley and Lucky

Dube serenaded each customer as they ate. Escoviche Fish dressed with vinegar, peppers and onions had just been put in the display case and the oxtails had simmered to "fall off the bone" tastiness. I was talking to a customer when Ms. Bailey, the landlord, walked in. She greeted me with a wave of her frail hand. I excused myself and went to meet her next to the juice counter.

"Hi, Ms. Bailey. Would you like some juice or a glass of water?' I asked, reaching overhead for a glass.

She spoke in a lethargic, high tone which seemed to screech over your ears, "Yes, Kim, carrot and apple juice, please."

Ms. Bailey was in her sixties. A petite white woman with dusty blonde hair, she walked as though one leg was slightly longer than the other, but she was very spry. She never bothered us while we renovated her place, and maybe she was just glad that we would be opening a restaurant. From time to time she would slowly ramble in and grin when she saw the restaurant was full, but I rarely saw her except on days when rent was due, and rent wasn't due for two weeks.

"So, how are you Ms. Bailey? Can I get you anything else?" I asked.

She reached over to touch the warmer where we kept the varieties of patties. "I'll take one of those filled with meat."

Not bothered by her mouth full of beef patty, she kept talking: "I wanted to let you know the other day when I was up in my apartment 'round four I smelled a very funny odor coming from the back of the restaurant in the alley. I couldn't tell what it was, but when I went to my window I noticed some of your staff out there just a giggling."

"Really," I replied. "What did it smell like?"

"I can't say. I didn't recognize it. I just noticed it smelled peculiar." Her barrage of words puzzled me, but I turned to look at my staff to recall who was working yesterday. "Well, thank you, Ms Bailey. I will look into it for sure. I appreciate you telling me, but I have to get back to the kitchen." I gave her a smile and went through the swinging doors to the kitchen.

Like clockwork the following day, I went out the door at 4:40. My normal routine would be to pick up Malcolm and drop him off with my grandmother until closing, but today would be different. On this occasion I called my grandfather to pick up Malcolm and I got in my car and drove around to the alley. I turned the car slowly into the narrow pass careful not to bear down on the gas pedal. As I approached the back of the restaurant, I saw four employees huddled together talking and smoking. I turned the car's engine off, quietly opened the door of the car, extended my leg gingerly onto the ground, and walked towards my wait staff. It didn't take long for the smell to dance around my nostrils before I knew what it was. Each one of my staff turned to look at me, the girls were smiling like Cheshire cats and the guys bugged, eyes heavy with blank expressions.

"What the hell are you guys thinking? Do you want to get me shut down? Is this what you guys do every day when I leave? What would make you think I would be cool with this?" My interrogation went on and on and my temperature kept rising until I felt my heart nearly jump out of my chest. I watched for their response and couldn't tell if it was the weed or my sonic blast of questions that had them dumbfounded.

Roxy, a beautiful, light-complected dread-locked sister on my wait staff, coolly turned her shoulders to face me and said, "We need to make the mood irie while we're working."

I wanted to laugh, just not to scream.

Needless to say, they were all let go before their buzz wore off.

RING

"Caribbean Cuisine, can you hold, please?" I put the receiver down while I served some customers. "Hello, Caribbean Cuisine, how can I help you?" I asked.

"Yea, hey baby, it's me, can you go to the airport and pick someone up for me? I'm coming in later this evening." Gbenga asked.

I heard the question, but couldn't find the right response.

"Can you do this?" his voice raised, the same time my patience gave in.

"No, I can't, as a matter of fact, I am knee deep in rice and peas and I had to let everyone go, except for the cook, for getting high in the alley"

CLICK! The phone went dead.

At that moment being hung up on didn't affect my mood one bit, because I was already thinking at hyper speed and my thoughts hadn't caught up with all the running I was doing. But as things slowed down and customers got up from their tables, I pondered the repercussions of my response to Gbenga. With each table I bussed, each ring the register made when the drawer came open, every dollar that I put into the register, every single curry stained table cloth I balled up to put in the linen bag, each shadow that passed over the front windows of the restaurant I grew more tense. The door swung open and my neck and eyes would turn towards the direction of the entry way, while my legs would shift my weight to the balls of my feet, prepared for agility.

The evening wore on and only the scent of crisp lemon zest wafted in the air, as we washed down all of the counters and got things prepared for the next day. The cook had left and I turned to hit the last light switch when someone grabbed me from behind. My legs were frozen and my pupils had not fully adjusted to the change in illumination. I felt my diaphragm muscles constrict as I prepared myself to scream, but the breath on the back of my neck kept me from any reaction. I had my keys in my left hand and used my thumb and index finger to push one single key between my fingers. I had gripped the key ring until I could feel my fingers go numb. I was preparing myself to gauge someone's eye out. Then, as if all of this was happening simultaneously, the next sound I heard was the cool tone of Gbenga' s voice and the aroma from the last drag he took off his cigarette. I stretched my finger-tips to catch the end of the light switch.

The light came on and I could tell by the scowl on his face that this was not going to be a welcome reception. I took time to choose my words. "Hey baby, why didn't you call me from the airport?" He took a step back, but didn't respond to me. "You tired? I'm going to get Malcolm, then we can go home and I will fix you something to eat." He still didn't say a word. A poison silence floated in the room. I wanted to kiss him, but my body was jumping inside, back and forth, up and down. I was scared the moment I put my lips close to him he would retort and slap me.

We rode to my grandparents' house without saying a word. I pushed in a Burning Spear reggae CD. hoping to calm his mood. I pulled into the driveway, but he didn't get out. Instead, he sat in the passenger seat and reclined. I picked up Malcolm and carried all of his toys. I got to the car and remembered the car seat was in the trunk. I asked Gbenga to open the trunk and help me with the car seat. He opened the trunk release switch from the glove box and came around towards me. I used one hand to open the trunk; he reached over the trunk and took Malcolm from my arms. I looked away and caught a glimpse of my grandmother standing in the doorway. Gbenga must have seen her too, because he quickly said in a loud voice; "Hi, Ms. G. I just got in and I'm still jet-lagged. Thanks for watching Malcolm."

My grandmother nodded and waved her hand as she closed the door. I put the car seat in the car and watched as Gbenga put Malcolm in and buckled him tight.

Finally home and my little boy was fast asleep. I carried him inside his carrier straight to bed. I went to my room and removed my shoes; I put one of my hands on the back of my neck to squeeze out the tension. I relaxed my eyelids and closed them. I moved my neck in circles, then opened my eyes and saw my Gbenga standing in the hallway looking at me.

"Why wasn't the car seat in the back of the car? You don't like people knowing you're a mother? Oh, no, I'm sure you prefer they just think of you as the pretty girl who owns the restaurant."

"I took the car seat out to load some cases of Ting into the back seat from Grandma's garage."

"What were they doing at your grandmother's house? Don't you have enough room in the restaurant? You sure there's no other reason?" His voice got louder and his eyes stared holes into mine.

"The delivery of drinks was going to be late, so I gave them her address." I responded, averting my eyes.

He opened his hand and swung to slap my face, I turned my head, but he still caught my face with the span of his fingers.

"Next time I call, you won't talk to me like I am somebody who works for you! You are always puttin' on airs, acting above your position. Do you think because you went to college you are better than me? Or is it because I am African?"

Immediately my chin rose to look into his face. "Don't you know that so many of the things I fell in love with in you are because you are African?

What kind of shit is that? Have I ever made a comment on you being African?" My thoughts trailed; how did he get me to go there, instead of mentioning his insensitivity to the long day I had? Wasn't it just that simple? My thoughts were interrupted…

"Why do you spend so much time at that restaurant? Who is raising my son? What is more important? Don't I provide for you? I helped you put that restaurant on a better level. Do you have someone coming to see you there? Is that it? You're a big business owner, so people want to fuck you, is that what has went to your head?" He went on and on shouting and shouting, his eyes wide and his shoulders leaning towards me. I sat on the couch melting deep into the cushions. I knew better than to answer. I had no idea what question to even address first. "Lord, bridle my tongue, Lord bridle my tongue" over and over, I repeated it in my head.

"What's wrong? You're not answering because you know I'm right." His voice raked over my eardrums and taunted me to retort. I got up to walk away. I didn't even want to look at him. I went to the bathroom and locked the door. I sat on the edge of the bathtub where I cried and prayed.

He must have given up banging on the door until the hinges nearly came off because after a while everything got quiet except the murmur of the television, so I came out. He was sleeping so quietly, his long eyelashes so feathery and thick against his brown skin. I stood there wondering what made him into the man he is? At that moment I knew I had to travel to Nigeria to meet his parents. If you want to know about the man, go look at the father, right?

For weeks Gbenga and I discussed the possibility of me visiting Nigeria. There were plans for me to make at the restaurant: more staff to hire, and decide who would be responsible for running it while I was gone. Gbenga had contacted his family about the visit. They sent long shopping lists of items they wanted from the United States for me to bring with me in my luggage. This was an exciting time. I had more questions with each day that passed. He and I seemed to be getting closer again, or at least we had something to focus on and talk about that would distract us from the problems at hand. Initially I believed he had reservations about my wanting to go to Nigeria, but after awhile he thought it necessary that I go so he could see my reaction to the culture.

Weeks passed and then months in preparation for this trip. I had received my passport and Malcolm's passport in the mail. The two of us had received our vaccinations and we were ready to make our reservations. I had run through all scenarios with the staff at the restaurant and I was confident that nothing bad would happen there during the week and a half we would be gone.

I went to visit my grandmother and I told her of my intention to travel. She sat at the table very quietly, weathered hands, with well manicured nails resting on her lap. "How long will you be gone?" she asked.

"A week and a half, or so," I said.

"What about the baby? Is it safe for him to travel with you? What about the restaurant?" The more questions she asked, the deeper the furrows became on her forehead.

"Yes, Grandma, we got our vaccinations the other day. He will be fine and Gbenga will be going in to check on the restaurant.

"You mean he is not going with you and the baby? Is it safe? Won't you get lost? Oh baby, I don't know if you should make this trip alone."

Her voice had a somber modulation: the excitement fell into concern. Her anxiety trailed through her parted lips and tapped at my back.

"Grandma, I will be fine. Malcolm will be fine. He is going to see his other grandmother and I am sure she feels just like you do and she wants to make sure we're safe too. With that, I told her how much I love her, gave her a hug, and we went out the door.

I could not find a seat in the boarding area for the flight to Nigeria, but today I was happy to stand. I hadn't even flown over African skies, and inside my stomach was an overwhelming sense of pride that caused me to stand up a little bit straighter. It felt so good to see all of the Black faces, different shades, dressed in different wrappings; some western, some traditional African, but all of the faces held warmth in their eyes. The stewardesses walked through and their blue uniforms and white skin looked paler against such a colorful backdrop of colorful people, amongst all of the black faces and colorful clothing. One by one all of the travelers picked up their hand luggage and large woven plastic bags to board the plane. I had a smile on my face as I handed the boarding passes to the KLM attendant. My excitement heightened with each step I took down the ramp to the plane. I held on to Malcolm, clutched him close to my chest and whispered, "We're going to Africa!"

The food on the flight was packaged on tiny trays, prepackaged and heated, chicken, rice pilaf with a fruit salad, a dinner roll and a small serving of a dessert that resembled custard pie. Wine is served with every meal, but I was still breast feeding Malcolm, so I drank luke warm ginger ale and kept the tiny wine bottles to give to family in Nigeria. The flight was seven hours, but I could not sleep. I reclined my chair and watched all of the in-flight movies. I looked over to Malcolm, eyes closed and lying quietly on the adjoining seat, and I wondered if he had any idea about the journey we were taking. My baby was no doubt an African American. With every strand of his DNA a cultural bridge was made. He would not have to read or speculate from a story what connected him to Africa besides his skin tone; he would grow knowing with all certainty that he did not have a watered-down culture; He would see his Africa, breathe it, taste it, all in a couple of hours.

I awoke to the sound of clapping and ringing in my ears. The plane had landed and the Nigerian travelers showed their appreciation to the flight crew by clapping to signal a safe landing. I looked out the window, and the airport appeared as any airport in the United States: paved runway, a small glimmer of lights along the sides could be seen through the glare of the sun. Large windows ran the length of the terminal and a large control tower could be seen in the distance. The sun had set, and the sky was a beautiful bouquet of sienna orange and powder blue. My wait was over: I was in Nigeria. I was in Africa.

I noticed the sweaters and jackets that had adorned the Nigerian travelers had now been tucked away. I now saw colorful fabrics on the women, made into beautiful blouses and long skirts, and heads that looked so regal swathed in fabrics embroidered with tiny metallic threads. Some men were still dressed in suits, while others wore elaborate fabrics of lace and brocade with bold embroidery around the neck and dropping to the chest, which draped pleat after pleat over the shoulder, cascading down to the floor, with matching pants, and colorful caps resting on their heads. As we walked off the plane I felt like I had walked straight into a fiery furnace. I put Malcolm down to walk, so I could remove his sweater and slip off my jacket. Tiny beads of sweat formed on my little boy's forehead as he walked through legs and luggage following behind us off the plane. I picked him up and noticed there weren't any people being received at the gate, so I walked holding Malcolm towards the sign that read "baggage claim". When we got to the end of the terminal, there were steps and an escalator that was not in motion, leading to a landing below. There were long lines for Nigerian citizens and foreign travelers. People stood in line holding passports and yellow customs declaration cards. My arms were heavy from carting Malcolm. The carry-on luggage was filled with gifts I had bought from the duty- free shops in Amsterdam, but a weight was lifted when I looked and saw all of the uniformed officers behind the immigration desks had black faces.

"Ah, my wife," the voice was thick drizzled with a British accent. I looked up to see who had spoken to me. "Yes, my wife, you are married to my brother, so you are my wife, welcome home," he said.

"Oh, thank you," I said and smiled. He was a customs officer, stocky in build, skin tone like oiled ebony and a small tribal mark etched on each cheek where dimples could have been. He stamped our passports and let me pass. I looked down at the baggage claim and then scanned my eyes among the shuffling people surrounding the two carousels that slowly moved. Gbenga told me his brother would be meeting me, but I had no idea what he looked like. Gbenga couldn't even describe him to me, because it had been over 17 years since he last saw his baby brother.

I kept my eyes on the carrousel as each bag came tumbling out. It moved very slowly, one piece after the other. The voices got louder as each bag was removed, falling with a loud 'thump' onto the baggage carts. Men embraced each other with loud boisterous greetings in different languages. The sounds caught Malcolm's attention and he clapped and waved his hands up in the air.

As I was looking through the crowd for Chike, Gbenga's brother, a young boy approached me.

"Let me help you with your bag." He said.

"I'm fine, really. I am waiting for someone," I said, picking up Malcolm and shifting him to my right hip.

"They will not allow anyone to come inside to meet you. I can take you outside. I work in the airport." He lifted up a laminated badge he was wearing around his neck with a picture of himself and green label which read "Federal Airport Authority Nigeria." "Your brother told me to help you."

I stopped and looked at him again, this time looking at his face and into his eyes "My brother is not here. I am waiting for my husband's brother. Where is he?"

"Oh yes, Madam, he is outside, I will help you with your bags." He spoke and reached for my carry-on luggage. Just then I turned to see a piece of my luggage coming around on the carousel.

"No, that's all right. I will pull this luggage. You can help me with the bag right there, the red one." I pointed at the red luggage that was approaching. I thought it was hideous when Gbenga had picked it out at the store, but now I was thankful because it was easy to identify.

The young man helped me put the luggage onto the baggage cart as we stacked one after the other, until three bags were on the cart.

"What do you have in these bags?" the young man asked.

"My clothes and gifts for my family."

"Do you have receipts for these gifts?"

"No." I thought to myself, how odd would that be carrying the receipts here with me. I looked at him through the corner of my eye.

"Well, Madam, you will have to put some money in your passport when you hand it to the officer, so he won't delay you in leaving," he said, as he started pushing the cart forward.

"Money?" I said. "How much money?" my "sista girl" voice started to come out.

"Well, madam, fifty dollars should be enough, but only a single bill. Just put it inside your passport and hand it to the officer."

"Fidy dollars?" Yes, I said 'fidy', the letters changing somehow in the language of "sista-girl." "I don't have fifty dollars, I have a twenty dollar bill and that will have to do, I don't mind waiting, I am not carrying anything in these bags that should concern anyone but me!"

From the look on his face he understood me very well, or he didn't want me to raise my voice, but either way he pushed the cart and headed towards the doorway.

"Ah, madam, welcome, what do you have in your bags?" the custom's officer questioned.

"Personal belongings," I replied, handing him my passport. He was dressed in a light brown starched uniform with a black beret tilted slightly towards his forehead. At least two other officers stood peering by his side. He opened my passport to look at my picture and coolly tucked the money under his fingers and into his palm. He glanced at Malcolm's passport and looked up at me.

"Oh, you are my wife, your husband is Igbo, nnon-o!"

I had no idea what he was saying, but I could tell it was a greeting of some kind in the Igbo language. I nodded my head and gave him a smile, then headed out through the door.

When I got through the door, what seemed like hundreds of people were waiting outside. Beautiful black faces in all shades, with beautiful teeth gleaming like stars in the evening light. Some were waving, a few held cardboard signs with names on them, most just gazing at each person as they came out the door. I was trying to take it all in, I felt the air embrace me. I took a deep breath and smiled, then released a part of me into the fragrant African air.

"Madam, whetin' for me?" The young man was talking, but I didn't want to lose the feeling of this moment, being in Africa. A man approached, about five foot ten, dark brown skin, with full lips that framed his smile nicely, but there was something about his eyes that was familiar; big brown eyes with long eyelashes that flashed as he smiled.

"Mama Chibu!" His arms opened as he got closer. I looked again, feeling a sense of familiarity.

"Chike?" He gave me a hug and looked at Malcolm. Chibu was the Nigerian name Gbenga gave Malcolm after consulting with his mother about his birth.

"Chibu, big boy, come see your uncle." He picked Malcolm from my arms and bounced him up and down. Malcolm seemed startled at first and then began to smile and laugh. "I just spoke to Gbenga. He told me what you were wearing, so I recognized you. Welcome, how was your flight?"

"It was nice, thank you, I am so happy to finally meet you." We walked and talked on our way to the car, my feet felt like they barely touched the concrete. I was so relieved that Chike was able to recognize me from my picture.

"Mama Chibu! Chibu boy, welcome, welcome!" I heard this voice, but could not see the face as I was lifted off the ground. When I came down a tall figure of a man with a face like Gbenga's came from behind me. I smiled and embraced him.

"This is Okey," said Chike, "my senior brother." I couldn't stop looking at him, the shape of his head, his expressions; all looked so much like Gbenga. I laughed inside to myself about how Gbenga would feel at the sight of his two baby brothers now grown men and resembling him.

All of a sudden my thoughts were broken by a loud argument between the young man that was pushing the baggage cart and my brother in laws. Okey was shaking his head, waving his hands and speaking in a different language. It turned out that neither Chike nor Okey had asked the young man to meet me inside the terminal, and now he wanted a tip, in dollars!

When it was all said and done Okey gave the boy who helped me with my luggage a few hundred naira, Nigerian currency, and told him he ought to go back to the customs officer for any balance he had coming to him. Annoyed, the boy balled the money into his inky black fist and walked away.

The warm breeze of the tropical climate felt good against my skin. We loaded into Chike's dust-blue Mercedes and headed to a nearby hotel.

The sun had set across a lavender-lit sky when my eyes settled on a vision I had never seen before. We were driving over a bridge when I looked down from the overpass to see a Black Exodus, thousands of people. Counting the whole population on the African continent, one –fifth of them are in Nigeria. There are 300,000 in downtown Lagos alone. All you could see for miles were black people: young, old, tall, short, fat, thin, blue-black, café au lait, and honey brown. Afro-beat music was playing, people were selling wares at their markets, small children with no shoes on ricocheted here and there. Mothers carried babies on their backs wrapped in bright fabrics exploding with colorful prints. Vendors carried large items on their heads; men stood alongside barbeque grills and sold roasted chicken or beef. It was a carnival in black.

"Where are we, Chike?" I asked, as I smiled. The window was all the way down.

"That's Oshodi market, the largest market in Lagos." He turned to look at me and then rolled up the window and turned on the air conditioner.

"Bolo, bolo, bolo!" yelled a small boy carrying peanuts wrapped in plastic baggies along with roasted plantains. He came to the window and pressed himself against the door. His big eyes and small frame startled me when I heard such a loud voice.

We rode along the freeway covered in darkness; the street lights were faint, like lightening bugs in an open yard. Third Mainland Bridge is what I read on the sign. Just underneath was the Atlantic Ocean, the keeper of so many souls who never made it on the journey through the Middle Passage. I stayed very quiet the rest of the way into the city. My heart was humbled looking at the black sky be-jeweled with all of its stars and the moon reflecting off the ocean, wondering with admiration at the strength it must have taken to endure such a life-altering journey.

We passed a large cargo ship docked at the opening of the city. Night cloaked the streets, yet they were still alive with people walking and riding small motorcycles, some three to a bike. Each corner had a steel drum barbeque pit roasting ears of corn or spicy-smelling meats over glowing embers. Women with powerful forearms sold bananas or popcorn on trays lit with homemade oil lanterns made from Peak evaporated milk cans, to passers-by headed home for the evening. I was so tired, but my excitement kept me awake. We reached the Federal Palace Hotel and drove up to the main lobby, where uniformed bell caps greeted us and took all of my bags. A couple of prostitutes lingered near the casino and they handed a well-suited man a business card. The lobby was gorgeous, African artwork, paintings, carvings and ivory sculptures all mingled with tall palm plants which decorated every corner. We approached the front desk, but Okey asked me to sit down on the lounge chair while they got my room. I looked behind the counter and noticed the framed pictures of two stately looking gentlemen dressed in military uniform decorating the walls. The writing underneath the pictures clarified that the two men were the Governor of Lagos State and the President of the Federal Republic of Nigeria. I could feel the corners of my mouth turn upward as I stood taller. "Yes, I am in Africa."

As we headed up the elevator to the room, it became clearer that the hotel charges two fees- the Nigerian fee and the foreigner fee. And that was my first taste of Nigerian irony, I was greeted as "my wife," but I was in a separate category. The night was long. We visited with relatives and guests and Malcolm beamed at all of the attention. He played for hours until his little legs couldn't carry him anymore. I will never forget my first trip, my first reaction of bright -eyed enthusiasm and optimism. I think I fell into a different kind of love and respect for Gbenga on that trip. I could see the lives he touched in Nigeria, the people he wanted to elevate if he was able. It was the drive behind his hustle.

*****

I was awakened by the low humming sound of Stacy's garage door opening. Enthusiasm burst through the door as her children bounced in talking of the adventures of the day. "Hey, Aunty!"

"Hi, beautiful. How was cheerleading?" I asked as I stretched my back.

"Cheerleading was good, did you cook anything?" her voice climbed as she went into the kitchen.

"Yes, there's macaroni and cheese with some greens cooking in the kitchen." Hearing the two of them stride like thunder up the stairs with their heavy feet only made me long for my boys. The giggles and the fighting back and forth reminded me of the questions that Steven would ask me, sometimes never stopping to breathe. Remembering the way my heart would sing to the tone of their voice when they would call for me. Mom, Mommy, I missed all of it. I wondered how they filled their days now. Who was Malcolm outrunning on the school playground, wearing his Corona School uniform checked with red and white and his loafers full of sand? I would see him and his friends under the huddle of banana trees in our yard discussing video games and soccer exploits. He has a smile that is contagious; you can feel his sincerity in every glimmer of his straight teeth. There has never been a time when I was hurting that Malcolm's smile didn't lift me up. Steven has a different approach; he has pools in his deep brown eyes that you fall into. He draws you in with overwhelming energy that goes on for days. He had the ability to reverse the effect of the tornadoes that sometimes consumed our house. Steven's energy at play was just as powerful; when he has drawn you to him, he grins, making his irresistible cheeks puff out and his dimples show. There was no doubt there was good inside Gbenga, because something bad could not produce such blessings in my life.

I felt my chest constricting, like the walls were closing in on me. The sight of Stacy's kids was making me miss my own so desperately. Their hugs would warm me, but I longed to be filled with the touch of my boys. I put on my shoes and asked Stacy to drop me off on her way out. I needed to get out of there.

My Grandma V is my maternal grandmother; short and stocky,

Filipina features, café au late complexion, with beautiful long salt and pepper hair. She is very sweet, but it is hard to know if you can get into her feelings. She talks with concern, but rarely leaves the comfort of her reclining chair which sits in her painted mustard yellow dining room in front of the TV., or the lounger which sits on her porch.

"Hi, Grandma V." I said as I leaned to give her a kiss.

"Oh, hi baby, have a seat. I'm watchin' my programs. How you doin'?" she asked, her eyes never leaving the television screen.

"I'm alright, Grandma, just missing the boys."

"You'll get those boys baby, you'll see." She turned to look at me and I sat down at the table. As I sat thinking of the possibilities, my uncle came up the stairs from the basement in his t-shirt and Dickey's.

"Hey, Kimmy, look at you all dressed up. Have you been out looking for a job again? You'll find one. You have a degree. Just give it time."

"The time just moves so slowly without the boys. But everyday I'm not with them, it seems like it's been eternity. I need to work and give my mind some more things to think about."

"Yes, well, Mr. 'Benji' called here this morning telling me how sorry he was for hitting you. He assured me that it won't happen again. I told him I better not see him over here with that mess, cos' you got family." His eyebrows rose while he was talking and he walked over to sit next to me.

"Thanks Uncle Paul, but it's not necessary and I doubt he will come here. He's got everything he needs there. He's got the boys." My thoughts drifted and I thought for a moment of how they were doing. What was their last thought of me? What was he saying to them about me?

*****

"Look at you, getting' dressed up so you can parade for those other men at your job," Gbenga ranted, glaring over at me as he lay on our bed half covered in the sheets.

"You get all dressed up just to leave the house. Who do you go see? Who are you fuckin' at your office?"

I stood there looking in the mirror at my navy blue suit at the hemline, at the space from my neck to the first button on my blouse. I couldn't feel the lining of my skirt against the curve of my hips, so I knew my skirt wasn't tight. I just stood distressed, not turning around. I tried to let his words pass without mumbling a word.

"Don't you know that's really all they notice in you? They only see a piece of ass. They just want to get in your pants. No one takes you seriously, just a piece of ass." He removed the covers and came out of the bed. The boys abruptly ran in the room, sharp-eyed with their school uniforms scattered and unbuttoned.

"You guys go and put on some lotion and I'll help you get ready in a minute so we can go." I touched Malcolm on his chin and gave Steven a kiss on the top of his head.

"Where the hell do you think you are going? You're not going back to that office. You have a choice: work or me." I listened for the soft trample of footsteps down the marble stairs, but noticed they stopped just past the first landing.

"Gbenga, this is not necessary, I'm going to work. I can't just walk out like that, no explanation. I asked you about working, before I took the job!" I leaned over to pick up my shoes from the floor.

"You see, you're a whore. Just look at how you are leaning over. I know you are fucking someone at the office. Is that what you are choosing?" He came close to me shaking his finger in my face, outrage seeping from beneath his fingernail. I recoiled, never fully straightening up my back as I turned to look at him.

"I don't know what you want me to do. They came to you before they offered me the job, I wouldn't put work before you, but I can't quit like that. Let me at least go and tell them I am leaving. But I still think we should talk about it." I walked towards the door and saw my babies in the hallway, quietly leaning against the wall. My heart crumbled. They didn't say a word, just looking up at me with beautiful eyes. I heard Gbenga walking towards the bedroom door, his slippers sliding against the marble floor.

The boys turned quickly to walk to their room. Steven looked up at his big brother and asked him, "What's a whore?" Malcolm didn't respond, but he turned to look at me; eyes obtruding through his narrow lids. Then he caught a glimpse of his father and turned away. Who knows what he is telling them now, but it's no worse than they have heard before.

*****

"See, Uncle Paul, it's not like he's a man taking care of children here in the States. In Nigeria he has a nanny, he has a cook, and he has a driver that can take them to school. It's not an issue of him getting worn down." I felt my heart race and crack at the same time. "What is he telling you? That he is sorry, when he knows why I left!"

"Kimmy, I think it dawned on him that you are serious. Gbenga said a lot of things to me this morning. Now, I am not saying to go back over there. I think he should come here if he wants to show you something. But I am saying he does realize the house is different now that you're gone."

My Grandmother V interrupted. "Now, I am not telling you what to do, but I do think you did the right thing. Those babies won't forget you. You know that you're living proof of a bond between a mother and a child. Look how you came back into our life. You didn't let adoption erase your mother from you. That was your momma!"

She had a point, or part of a point, but she had no idea what drew me to my natural mother. It really wasn't out of love. How could I love someone I never knew? She was a mystical fragment of a family I longed to be a part of, appearing by osmosis, frequently returning to my dreams. I saw the two of us in a couple of pictures when I was a few months old, but I didn't want to see her out of love. I wanted to see her because I had questions to ask, which only she could answer for me. I carried that hurt around for a long time. I wanted to see her because any time I didn't follow my

scented dryer sheets, rubber bands grouped around ten-thousand-dollar bundles, each separated in hundred dollar groups, tens, twenties, fifties, hundreds. I would sit and count every bill until my hands hurt, keeping the final number in my head.

Gbenga would come in town, usually just with a carry-on or a leather garment bag filled with designer suits. He stopped asking me to come and pick him up at the airport and preferred to take a taxi to the house or to the restaurant. He said it was not to inconvenience me, but I knew he just had trust issues and preferred to show up announced. Whenever he came to the restaurant he would sit at that same dimly lit table, scanning a newspaper, attentive to everyone who came in the door. But his posture was different, fluid, each position choreographed, steady. He answered his cell phone, finished his call, lit a cigarette, and even the smoke was orchestrated when to leave sight. When someone came to his table, he never moved an inch. He seldom smiled, but when you saw it, it was like the sudden blue flame from a struck match in a black room- warm, inviting, but fleeting. Later he would go out to Easton Mall or out with various African friends and come back late in the evening.

From time to time he would get to the house before me and a strange car would be in the garage. The first time I saw an unfamiliar car my heart was racing. I couldn't reach him on his phone. I would page him and put in my code with 911, 911. He didn't call. I waited outside for twenty-five minutes with Malcolm in the backseat. Finally I got out of the car, picked up Malcolm from his toddler seat and took him by the hand while I slowly opened the door. I walked inside. I heard music playing softly down the hallway, but saw no one. Trailing the sound, I went to the room and opened the door. There was an automatic hand gun lying on the bed. I was hearing something rustling on the floor. I coolly walked around the bed.

"Hey baby." Gbenga said looking up, while he was sitting on the floor.

"What the hell is wrong with you?" I asked as I turned and slammed the door behind me. I turned on the VCR in the living room and sat with Malcolm on the couch. We sat there singing and playing with the animation on the television until he was asleep. I went back to the bedroom, where Gbenga was now standing beside the bed. The gun was gone.

"Gbenga, whose car is in the garage?"

"Oh yea, it's a rental."

"Well, why didn't you answer my call when I called you?"

"I didn't see the phone ringing. It was on vibrate," he said, never looking up at me, concentrated on the package in front of him.

"Do you realize all kinds of things were going on in my mind when I pulled up to the house?"

"Sorry, baby, I was packing something. I didn't hear the call."

I moved closer and for the first time, saw what he was wrapping on the floor. It wasn't money. There were nearly two dozen packages. Each packet was solid white, maybe the size of a three- ring day-timer, with a funny symbol stamped on the outside latex covering. I didn't have to see the inside to know what it was. They were bricks of dope and this was my first time seeing them up close and out of the luggage. I touched them and tried to imitate how Gbenga was handling them. I forgot how angry I was, how scared I was. He handed me a package and asked me to wrap it for him: downy sheets, cellophane, and packing tape. Wrapped up, it was easy to forget this stuff was just pretty poison. Funny how each package seemed to be a bit symbolic. On the surface one could see powder-white, seductive with fair innocence, but get it in your system and this stuff could make empires cripple and collapse until there is nothing left but rubble and remembrances of what once was. I picked up those bricks and wrapped them the same way I had been picking up the pieces of myself each day with Gbenga, forgetting just how toxic our relationship was. He must have been comforted by my willingness to "be down." I thought it was no different than what I had been doing for months, I knew what he was doing, and by choosing to do nothing I was just as involved. He took me in his arms, drawing me hard and quickly into his body. I was pulled in by his extrinsic scent, the musk, the Cartier fragrance taunting me to inhale, closing my eyes until my lungs were full. My lips were full of heat and every hair on my body was responsive to his slightest movement. I forgot about everything else but the slow burn of him inside me, igniting the sweetest response from my head to my toes, until everything sparked from the blaze. The feeling was familiar and intense. I wasn't ready to let it go. I thought I could control it, so I rolled him over, and slowed down the momentum stroking with a soft thrust, to the deep bluesy voice of Mary J singing in the background. I slid down to take him in my mouth, licking and sucking until I could feel his balls get hard, like they were ready to burst. I stopped wanting the control and just wanted to feel the engaging paradox of a cool river sending fire through my body. I mounted him, the numbness of him flowing deep inside of me. He was my drug.

I got up from the chair at my grandmother's dining table and took a deep breath. "What did we build, Gbenga? What was it that we built? Every day we were together there were parts of our lives that were hidden. Everything I did, I did only to show you I was on your team, that I loved you. I followed you, I never asked to lead. I just wanted you to love me back, but it never occurred to me who or what was leading you!" The words jumped out of my throat the same time the tears welled up in my eyes.

"I know baby, I'm sorry. Let me make it up to you."

"I am tired, Gbenga. Nothing I seemed to do could show you how much I loved you. I sacrificed my dreams, my restaurant, my life for you, and for what? Now I'm ten years older, and life is not waiting on me!"

"I know. Please, we can work this out. I will go to church, we will go together. Just come back. Let me show you I have changed. I need you. The boys miss you."

That was the defroster, I wondered if the boys were standing there listening to one end of the conversation, hearing their Daddy pleading with me and thinking I wasn't giving our family a chance.

"Could you please put them on the phone?" Grabbing a tissue from the table I quickly blew my nose.

"Hi Mom." Steven's voice was light, but very clear. I felt the tears rolling faster down my cheeks as I smiled.

"Hi, baby, how's Mommy's big boy?" My chest was tight and my breathing very short, trying to hold back my tears.

"Mom, when are you coming back, Mommy?"

I wanted to gather him up through the phone and hold him close to my chest. I missed the way his soft hands would squeeze the soft part on the back of my arms. I imagined those deep brown eyes and long fluttering eyelashes looking up at me.

"Baby, I can't say right now, Daddy and I are trying to work some things out." The words sounded so feeble to me. It didn't touch the surface of what was happening.

"I miss you, Mommy. Esther can't make pancakes." Simple words from my baby tore open my soul. I sat down barely able to hold the phone to my ear, the receiver sliding off my chin, wet from tears.

"I'm sorry, baby. Mommy will talk to her. I promise when I see you I'll make the best pancakes you have ever tasted." I heard a sigh when he breathed, like a smile was breaking through. I remember his smile, his cheeks so soft and full, his dimples on each side, kissed by me a million times. "How is school, Steven? How is your friend Abayome?" The question came out so odd to my ears. How could I be asking him about school? I had dropped him off every morning, each of his teachers knew me by name, and I never missed a parent-teacher conference or program. And now I am a spectator.

"School's fine. I love you, Mom. Here's Malcolm." He dropped the phone so suddenly, the way he had started to break out of my arms now that he was older and loved to run.

"Mommy," Malcolm's voice was dull and flat. My mind reflected on the day before we packed to leave. I could see the iridescent ribbons on his cheeks where his tears had dried, as he slept balled up in his bed.

"Hi, Malcolm. I miss you so much."

"Mommy." The tone in his voice was so stoic. I straightened up and wiped my tears so I could detect his every syllable.

"Baby, I'm here. What is it, Malcolm? Talk to me."

"Mommy, you know my birthday is in a couple of weeks. Mom, you've always been with me on my birthday." The phone went silent, all but the hum and the static over the phone line. I tapped my foot over and over on the hardwood floors, hoping the vibration would stir some insight into my next statement. I took a deep breath.

"Malcolm, I know and I think of that every day it gets closer to your birthday. You know why I left, don't you?"

"Yeah, I know," There was a slight whine in his response.

"Then you also know that I can't say when I am coming back.

Your Daddy needs to know what he did was wrong. Don't you remember our talk about choices and consequences?"

"I know, but Daddy promised me he wouldn't hit you again. He promised me." He seemed convinced that those words would make it all right. I knew he remembered waking up to the sound of hands smacking against skin, the muffled sounds of pushing in the dark, the echoing of loud voices arguing over work, jealousy, dinner, a shirt that was left at the drycleaners. Certainly, the sight of his father pressing his lit cigarette into the back of my neck as I lay cowering in a ball trying to make myself small enough where I couldn't even see myself on the bed screaming had been buried in his mind with some of his other feelings. That night he cried for the fighting to stop, until his eyes were red with rage. That night, he balled up his tiny fists and punched his father from behind until he let go of me.

"Do you believe him, baby?" I was asking him for his thoughts, but I was pulling him in to give me some type of assurance. Isn't that what I was trying to relieve him from? He was weeks away from being ten years old and I was asking him to reassure my safety.

"Mommy, he told me he wouldn't. He promised." The tone of his voice changed.

"Malcolm, I love you so much, I would never want to miss your birthday. There are some things your Daddy and I need to work out. It's not that easy. Please give me some time. Say your prayers and call me in a few days. I love you. Please know that I am always with you. There's a scrapbook in your closet that I had been making for you. Please take it out and read it, so you know not a day goes by when you're not on my mind."

The tears kept falling as quickly as I could get my words out. Sorrow was seeping through my pores and seizing my liveliness.

"I love you Mom, Mom…"

Nothing was left in me to come out. I sat there with my head bowed and mouth open, wanting to speak, but everything stood still, my voice lost in the hollow of my heart. I heard a rustling over the phone.

"Kim, baby, look, don't say anything. I know it's hard. I know it will be hard to look at your family and tell them you are coming back here, but this is where you belong. You belong here with us." Gbenga's voice, that syrupy manner washed with African intonation, drifted into my eardrum. I just wanted my babies.

"Gbenga, honestly, we have been working at this thing for years. Well, I have been working at this thing; you have just been working. And I am not saying work is altogether bad, but whom are you working for? I moved to Nigeria with you because I was so happy that you wanted to stop living a life in the game. I always knew you had more in you than that. I was hoping the move would give us a better chance to get over hurts and have a life together. The money would come. Instead, we spent years living in the same house, but rarely in the same room. I don't want what this has turned into. I am scared of you. I don't know you! How can you say you love me and you hit me, kick me, burn me? The bruises all eventually fade, but so does your own memory of ever hurting me. You can't see fractured bones under my skin, so you pretend they are not there. I can't live like that anymore. I see those scars every day. The pain is still with me. Make up doesn't hide everything. Multiply that by the fact I was thousands of miles away from my family. Like you used to say to me: it would be weeks before anyone would find my body!"

Gbenga interrupted. "I know, baby. I look at myself and I don't know what had come over me. Please, come home and let me make it up to you. Just show me this gesture of faith in us and I will prove to you it is a good decision."

"Gbenga, I don't trust you, and quite frankly you must not trust me, or you wouldn't constantly accuse me of being with other men. Do you really think I would follow you all the way to Africa to find another man? You would send me to go and speak to other men to get contracts and in the same breath tell me I was fucking them to get it! Here it would be a shame I could move from, there it's a disgrace I could never pay. And why would I stay with you, if it wasn't because I loved you? If you think it was for the money, that's a joke. I had my hands on mad money, but I never took a dollar, not one kobo!"

"I can't say anything else from here, other than I love you. You are good for me, the best part of me. I give you my word that I won't hit you again."

"I've heard that before, and anyway it's the Embassy that helped me leave and they have my passport until I can pay them back their money.

I have been looking for a job since I came back, but it hasn't been easy. I've been gone for so long."

"Leave the job. Don't continue to look for another position. I will send you the money to pay the Embassy. Get another passport and come back to your home. If you don't trust me, trust that God would put you at peace if you were meant to stay where you are."

An influx of emotion whirled around my head like a tornado, throwing feelings around like debris caught up in the eye of the storm. I knew how easy it was to get entranced by Gbenga. He reads people for weaknesses. He is capable of making you second guess the things you know to be true. He has a lure that can pull you in; not with the comfort of an embrace or hug, but closeness with a feeling of cold isolation when someone is staring down your back.

"Please let me speak with Malcolm." I wanted to hear my baby's voice, so my mind could focus and my thoughts would stop spinning.

"Mom?"

"Malcolm, there is nothing I wouldn't do for you. I want you to know I will think about what you said. I never set out to be away from you, but there is a lot to consider. Take care of your brother, and try to call me soon. I love you." I hung up the receiver and sat motionless in the chair. Was this just my cross to bear? Where was the place in me where I loved this man so much that I had no room left to love myself? Where did it happen? When was that moment? How did I get there?

10 Stiches on Snitches

I stood over the stainless steel sink in the back of the restaurant cleaning out the mop bucket, watching the sand and dirt whirl round and around down the drain with the water. The smell of bleach and detergent wafted in the air carried by thick steam clouds from hot water. I was at a crossroads. My son was growing every day, but his Daddy heard about most of it over the phone. My restaurant was blowing up, and so were the propositions from men who wanted to share in my success. What once seemed flattering had quietly become 'my options.' Then I thought of the mule that was lying up in the Radisson hotel, still sleeping I'm sure, covered in a plush white down comforter, waiting for me to pick her up and take her to the airport. Something needed to change. Something needed to be cleaned out of my life, down the drain.

I went to my purse and brought out a stark white business card. Mark Ratner, Drug Enforcement Agency. I thought about the one night when I was pulling up at an afterhours Reggae club on Mount Vernon Avenue on a Friday night to deliver food, when I noticed some vans pulling up around the backside of the building. I turned off my headlights, but I stayed in the car. Nine minutes passed, and like roaches when the lights are turned on, people scurried everywhere. I didn't move. I just watched as people were escorted into waiting vans, while others were thrown onto the brick wall outside as cocky undercover officers and overzealous alphabet boys yelled and went through pockets. My attention was on the circus of festivities, when out of nowhere a man rashly got into the backseat of my car. My pulse quickened, but it was too quick for me to respond. I felt his arm reach over the back of the car seat. I turned my head to the right, and saw a white man dressed in all black with a black ball cap which read DEA.

"Can I help you?" I asked, unclipping my seat belt.

"I don't know, you might. I guess you came too late," he exclaimed with a placid smirk on his face.

"No, it looks like I came right on time. I don't know what I'm going to do with this food, though." I heard the sound of foil paper as it was pulled back from the pan.

"Smells good."

"Look, unless you are buying it or you want to ask me about my vending license, I suggest you step out of my car." I looked around to get a really good look at his face. I had seen this guy before.

"No, I know you got a license, Kim. I know you own a restaurant.

I would like to ask you some questions, though, so call me." He handed me a card and blew out of the car, just as he came in, taking a beef patty with him. Studying the acronym on his jacket, I watched him as he got into the back of one of the vans and rode off.

I drove to a pay phone that night, rifled through my glove box, found a calling card and spoke to Gbenga. I was spooked and convinced he needed to get out of the game. Our conversation never came to a resolution, but I did get the impression that he felt his "business" was more viable than my restaurant. I was proud of my accomplishments. I was comfortable making a profit of about $70,000 a year, I didn't owe anyone. But he made that in a month. If we worked together, I knew there was room for growth and expansion, but I think he saw the restaurant as a hobby. I had never given that business card a second thought until now.

I showed up at the office of the Drug Enforcement Agency with my lawyer, Mr. Schwartz, and a briefcase full of paperwork. Myron Schwartz was one of the fiercest lawyers in town. An old Jewish man with wiry white hair, well dressed, but shoes that were run over and could use a good polishing. It wasn't really what I imagined when I walked in, but I introduced myself and handed the lady behind the reception desk Mr. Ratner's card. Walking in with a dark suit and tie on was Mr. Ratner. At that moment I knew where I had seen him before. He was the man I had seen over a year earlier across the street from the restaurant one evening as I was closing.

"Kim, I appreciate you coming in."

"This is my attorney, Mr. Schwartz. He'll be sitting in with me, since you didn't tell me the basis of the questioning." Mr. Schwartz extended his hand and followed us back to the office.

"Kim, a lawyer wasn't necessary," Mr. Ratner leaned into me, lowering his voice.

"Well, no one has ever approached me the way you did. Makes you wonder…" We entered a conference room that had a two way mirror on the right side of the room. Mr. Ratner left and came back in with a pasty white gentleman with brown oily hair in a gray suit, who didn't introduce himself.

"I'm here, so maybe you can tell me what you wanted to talk to me for?" Mr. Schwartz put his hand on my knee under the table to calm my aggression. The other guy reached under his arm for a folder and slapped it down on the table.

"Do you know Samuel Fisher?" Mr. Ratner opened the folder and placed in front of me a picture of a tall thin dark-skinned man with a thick goatee. I had seen his face before, but I couldn't place who he was.

"Nope, don't know him. Should I? I looked up at the anonymous man standing by the table.

"How about some of these people? Do you know any of them?" I looked through all of the pictures. None caught my attention, except one: Gbenga.

"Yes, I know this one, why?"

"How do you know him?"

I looked at my lawyer and he nodded his head. "I said I know him, but before I answer any- thing further I want to know why you are asking me these questions?" Mr. Ratner got up from his seat and came around the table towards me with a scowl on his face.

"You see this man?" pointing to the man with the goatee. "He is under a secret indictment for selling heroin. Someone who works for him sold to an undercover policeman and now he is working for us on the street". I crossed my legs and leaned back into my chair. "Wrong guy, wrong drug," I thought to myself. I moved closer and looked closely at the pictures.

"We know you know some of the people in these pictures!" His tone was hard and aggressive.

"You know what, you're right. I never said that I didn't. But what has it got to do with me?" My back straightened as I uncrossed my legs and looked him in his face. The thought had crossed my mind before I came in there that Gbenga could be involved. There were nights that I stayed in bed late after a fight, body bruised, head ringing, when I wondered: was he shot, was he dead, did he go to jail? But this was never a circumstance I wanted him to be in. I wanted him to stop hurting me, but I never wanted harm to come to him.

"Doesn't this picture look familiar?" He turned over a picture of

Gbenga and me coming out of Ashley's Jazz Club. It made me laugh because it looked like one of our happier moments.

"Mr. Ratner, this is silly. That is me and the father of my child. Now last time I checked, that was not a crime." I turned to Mr. Schwartz.

"Gentlemen, I think this has taken up enough time and my client showed good intentions to cooperate in coming down here. There has been no basis shown that would lead to this questioning or her involvement, so we are going." Mr. Schwartz stood up and nodded for me to stand.

"Where did you get the money to open your restaurant Kim?"

"Mr. Ratner, I was fully prepared and anticipating that question. Are you making allegations to illegal funds?"

"Benji has ties to a known heroin kingpin. We have intercepted several people in the last year that have been used as mules, swallowing packages of heroin and bringing them into the country. Some of them were not lucky enough to survive. He knows this man and so do you!"

"I don't know him. I have seen him. Most Nigerians here know each other- they eat at the same little spots, they might speak the same language, or shop at the same stores. But I couldn't tell you his name. Benji isn't involved in heroin, so you are making a wrong connection. As for where my money came from, it is all here- bank statements, grant approvals, awards and tax documents. I pay my accountant before I pay myself. I know I am a young Black woman doin' things, and I am sure that blows your mind, but it's me, it was made legal, and it's real. I worked hard for this. Don't you dare take away what I have built, as a fluke!"

I placed a large binder on the table and took back my seat. Mr. Ratner didn't say a word and his colleague stood, hands crossed, in silence. I had a renewed confidence because I knew all of my books were clean.

"I think this is over, gentlemen. Here is my business card if you have further questions." On that note we left. Mr. Schwartz picked up my financial documents and turned to look at Mr. Ratner.

"You can call my office if you would like a notarized copy of these. Please make sure it is accompanied by a warrant or an order from the court."

I learned something about drug investigators that day: most of their leads come from guesses and informants, rarely from facts. They didn't have their information right, but it was enough for me to know Gbenga did not need to continue life in the game. I talked to Gbenga later that evening and he said he was coming to town the following day.

*****

Gbenga sauntered into the restaurant as the dinner crowd was filing out. He sat at a table, cigarette in hand, and orders brown stew fish from the waitress as she passes by the table. I am talking to Bryce, this fine looking Polynesian guy who comes in to eat with his dad a couple times a week. I leave the table and notice Gbenga behind the bar changing the music on the sound system. I go over to greet him, but he takes my hand and releases it coolly as he comes around the bar. I tried to look into his eyes, but they lowered half mast and turned towards the table. I could sense the tension creeping over my body and propping on my shoulders. I attended to each customer serenely, clearing every piece of silverware, removing the white tablecloths, and wiping down every table. The waitress had just returned the handbill containing the credit card to the last customers. As they stood to leave I walked over to them carrying baked pineapple topped with honey and shredded coconut. This was a delicacy I usually only offered to large groups or for celebrations, but this was a different occasion: I was stalling an inevitable confrontation.

The customers had gone and the wait staff muffled around, stacking chairs and steam mopping the floors. I slipped behind Gbenga and started to caress his earlobes between my thumb and forefinger. My hand trailed the breadth of his chest leading my body in front of him. He sat leaning back in the chair, his expression just hanging on his face. He cocked his head and looked at me sideways. I had seen this look so many times before. It was dark and unyieiding. Sometimes, I could feel it when it wasn't piercing from his eyes. It shifted along the aisles of the grocery store and peered through the branches of trees, waiting, studying me.

"Hey, baby. Let's leave Malcolm at Grandma's for a little while and go catch a movie?' "You've been away from him all day. He needs to be picked up."

"We will pick him up, but I haven't seen you in awhile. Let's just spend some you and me time." I rubbed my hands on his head, massaging my fingers through his fade.

"Let's pick him up and go home." His voice was daunting, as he rose from the chair.

"Peter, please lock up. I'll see you tomorrow." I turned to grab my bag from the bar and we left.

I drove straight to my grandmother's house without muttering a word. I could still feel the tension leaking all over the car. I rolled the window down to get some air. My hands were sweating on the steering wheel. At this point I wasn't sure if I should talk about my meeting with the DEA or not.

"Did you want to know what happened downtown?" I asked.

"I want to know what made you set an appointment with them in the first place?"

"I thought it's better to know what they know, than to be in the dark."

"If they had anything, they wouldn't have invited you. They would come and pick you up." He looked at me with a vacant expression, his lips curled up and head tilted sideways.

"Yeah, maybe you are right, but I don't like living out an episode of Fear Factor and I don't want any unnecessary heat coming to the restaurant. So I went with Myron. He didn't seem to think it was a bad idea."

"Of course he doesn't. If you get locked up, it's a big retainer for him. He wins either way."

"Well, I can tell you and I are not on the same page, but I think you should know what is happening. Black is under a secret indictment for a heroin charge, and I get the impression they are trying to build a stronger case against him. They had pictures of some Nigerians, you, and one of me and you coming out of a club. So at least you should know to be careful." My eyes never left the road, so I couldn't read his expression until he spoke. Then I thought for a moment. The way he nonchalantly mentioned me being locked up, what, was he crazy? Was I crazy?"

I pulled into the driveway at my grandparents' house. I rang the doorbell and I heard Malcolm's footsteps and his laughter as he ran towards the doorway. My grandma answered the door and asked me to come in. She looked to the car and noticed my headlights were still on.

"Is your car running baby? You know that's unsafe."

"Oh thanks Grandma, but Gbenga is in the car."

"Gbenga?" my Grandfather interrupted. "Why is he always sitting in the car? Tell him he needs to come in this house and speak."

I took Malcolm in my arms and walked with him outside.

"Gbenga, my grandfather wanted to speak with you, can you please come inside?"

"I smell like cigarettes, Kim. Can you tell him that I am tired from my flight?"

"Gbenga, come inside. You know it's disrespectful. I won't tell him anything. You can stay out here if you want, but we're going inside."

Malcolm grabbed his daddy by the hand and walked him in the house. My grandfather, a tough-minded man, met us in the dining room and asked Gbenga to sit down.

"Hi, Gbenga. It seems I don't see you very often anymore. Are you working a lot lately?" Gbenga reared into the couch, sinking into the cushions. "No Sir."

"Well, if you are not working so much, then why do you spend so much time away?"

Gbenga went into his whole explanation about his job and his plans. I sat quietly on the chair in the dining room wondering if my grandfather's inquisition would yield any more answers than I had gotten over the last four years. They went on and on talking while I was asking my grandmother about Malcolm's day and telling her about the interesting things that happened at the restaurant. She and I were laughing when I noticed there were no other voices other than our own.

"It seems you need to make a decision, Kimmy, to be a wife and a mother, or a career woman." My grandfather, seventy nine years old, sat with his arms crossed, looking over the back of his armchair at me.

"What is wrong with what I am doing now? It took me a lot of work to own a restaurant. Why can't Gbenga move?"

My grandfather looked at me and slowly rose from his chair. "You are a mother, and you need to make a home for Gbenga to lay his head before he finds somewhere else to lay his head."

My grandmother came out from the kitchen and stood beside me. She raised her left hand to her face. It was the only thing preventing her jaw from dropping to the floor. I grabbed her hand and stood to my feet. Gbenga sat there pushed back into the couch, not saying a word. I don't think he felt he had to.

"You decided to have a family, now you need to decide to keep them together." Grandpa got up, looked at Malcolm, then looked over at me.

I watched Gbenga closely. He didn't budge. My grandfather had no idea what truth he was basing his judgments on. The restaurant not only brought in good money, but it was honest money. Gbenga didn't say one damn word. He wasn't going to, and he was confident I wouldn't either. My grandparents raised me in the church. I ought to know betta. I was the hope- the one who went to college. Gbenga watched me stand with my mouth closed. I couldn't speak. If I did, it would still fall back in my face. 'Well, you were the one who laid up with a dope dealer.' I looked into my grandfather's face hoping he would see my hard work and success, hoping there was some trace of approval between the folds in his forehead. There was nothing.

I looked over at Malcolm, playing with one of his cars. I picked him up and looked into his sweet face. He wasn't a baby anymore. He was losing more than his baby fat. He was losing every day he didn't have with his father. I didn't want my gain to be his loss. I didn't want Malcolm to feel "less than" because he didn't grow up with a Mommy and a Daddy. Not if I could help it.

*****

Malcolm and I played on the floor and listened to music. I could tell he was getting very sleepy, so I carried him over to his Daddy on the chair. They talked and rocked back and forth, until I couldn't tell which one was putting the other to sleep. I slipped into the bathroom to take a shower, allowing the jets to lightly tap my shoulders. I called to see if Gbenga wanted to join me. There was no response. I got out wet and opened the door to call his name. I didn't see anyone sitting in the chair. I heard a voice coming from Malcolm's room. I went to the room and saw a tiny light flashing in the dark. Moving closer, I could see Gbenga on his cell phone. He quickly closed down the top to his phone and turned towards me. Suddenly the air grew thin; my breathing was strained. Signals came off Gbenga's body, deliberate, but without movement, like pupils dilating. My sixth sense was on point and it told me there was a woman on the other end of that phone.

"Who was that?" Funny how we ask questions that we know the answer to, but we leave an opening for a possible escape.

"One of my boys." He walked right passed me. I was drippin' wet and naked. I couldn't tell if he was fleeing the question or not happy with what he saw. In any case, it felt like I had been discarded. On one hand my suspicions supported my confirmation for keeping my restaurant. Then there was the other hand: if I was wrong, I was denying my son a father. This was an out, which I twisted into a challenge.

"Gbenga, the restaurant is doing well, it's taken time to grow, money is coming in, we're getting good coverage."

"Don't you mean you are getting good coverage?" He remarked, lying on the bed looking up at the ceiling.

"Coverage, I haven't gotten any coverage from you since you've been in town. All this stuff and media attention going on, and to top it off I'm being told running the restaurant is making me an irresponsible mother and an undesirable candidate for a wife. My grandfather, the very man who gave his blessing on our relationship, pending our marriage before Malcolm was born, now feels it's my ambition that is keeping you from doing what is right. It is you not doing what is right that makes me desire the security of my own business."

None of my words or my dreams appeared to move him in the slightest. We lay in bed two visitors, miles apart between every thread count woven in the sheets. I have no idea when I finally went to sleep, but I woke to an empty bed, dull whispers stirring from the front of the house. Still nearly naked, the vulnerability of the climate provoked me cover up with Gbenga's t-shirt, the smell of Cartier filtering onto my skin. I entered the hallway…

"I'll be damned," I said to myself as the whispers stopped and click, the phone closed. I stopped short of the living room, hot breath coming from my nose and bitterness clutching my throat. Gbenga came around the corner. I was looking for something in his eyes. He passed, a holograph, void, passing through me. I pulled a deep intonation from deep down beneath my heels.

"Gbenga, who are you talking to? Do you want to be somewhere else?" Thoughts were competing for space in my head, somewhere underneath that. Sound was racing to catch up to the thoughts. Then my emotions and dashes of rational thought went numb, bringing deafening white noise and a reticent shift in my ambition. I forgot the sense behind what I knew was on the other end of that phone, and the desire to hold on to my relationship ate up my desire to build up the restaurant.

What happened in the next couple of months was dreamlike. The lunch hours were filled with swarms of people; pots bubbled and boiled over with oxtails and brown stew fish. The gumbo we added to the menu during the winter sold out every afternoon around two. My cook was always late because the pending close of the restaurant meant drastic changes for him too. His working visa lay in the balances; so did his living arrangements. His answer--- find some little honey he could marry so he could stay in the U.S. But he didn't dip his finger in- he went through the whole honey pot. One after the other they trailed in to the restaurant: white girls, black girls, one Asian girl, and one girl so big that when she held him only his feet gave clues that she was concealing a man beneath her arms and her breasts.

Caribbean Casanovas spent unhurried sips over bottles of Ting trying to bag me, thinking they could have the restaurant. Offers came in from other owners to buy the kitchen equipment, the furniture, even the lighting fixtures. I was becoming sentimental about utensils and laminated lunch menus. I straightened every tablecloth each night, taking every opportunity to sit in each chair and have a meal. At nights I would pick up Malcolm and bring him to sit with me at the juice bar. We would eat plantains and laugh while drinking cream soda, his chubby legs hanging over the barstool.

"SOLD!" The auctioneer from Wasserstrom repeated over and over after bantering prices to a packed house of vultures. Stuff was moving all around me and I couldn't dull my other senses long enough to focus on who was getting what. When I finally cleared my eyes so I could see and not shed tears, I noticed my accountant walking to the dining section. "None of this is for sale."

"Are you sure? There are some people over there who said they would pay five times what it was worth." The auctioneers' face was open; his mouth parted and his eyelids stretched.

I walked over to Mr. Lampkin, my accountant. "Not this stuff, this stuff has value to me."

The auctioneer walked toward the waiting group, two of them holding check books. I noticed their faces. They weren't restaurant owners. Most were customers I served many times, some as far back as when I was the only one doing the cooking.

"Kim, hi, I know this is probably not the best time for you, but I wanted to ask if you were open to selling any of those t-shirts or old menus?"

"You know what, sir? Every item that is being carried out of here goes with a piece of me.

I sweated, toiled, and laughed among every oven, every utensil, every pot, every thread in the Berber carpet. These menus are very valuable to me. They let me know that I could do it, and I am leaving because I want to, not because I failed." He nodded, clasping the hand of the woman beside him.

"You should always know that this was a special place to a lot of people, the food and the atmosphere. Thank you, because this is where we had our first date, our first kiss, and the place I said yes I would be his wife." She looked into up into his eyes, and him endearing into hers. I was hoping to be walking into that kind of love. I picked up two shirts and a menu, and handed it to them, the woman hugged me, her eyes glassy, as one tear fell onto her cheek. Her husband reached into his pocket and extended his hand holding two hundred dollar bills.

I held his hand closed inside both of my palms, "I'm glad this place will always have a connection with you, no thanks needed. God bless."

The once bubbling kitchen was empty and solemn; I felt lost, emotions bouncing around in a linoleum sanitarium. I left the small radio on in the staff room, a Marcia Griffith's song was playing; "When Will I See You Again". I locked the door, crossed the street and watched the awning in my rear view mirror until I turned on Fifth Avenue to get on the expressway.

Like Glue

Seasons don't really change much in Houston. I enjoyed weekends in Galveston on the beach, and lunch at Kim Son's restaurant on Fondren, but moving in together meant more and more time apart. I would cook meals that would go uneaten. Gbenga would come into the house, only to go upstairs with friends to play pool and speak in languages I struggled to understand. A couple of nights a week he would leave for "business" and come in after midnight. I would stay up looking out the window, waiting for his friend Jide to drop him off. His touch became very mechanical, his words uncomforting.

"What did I move here for? Why did I close the restaurant?" I gazed at him from the kitchen as he came in carrying logo steeped shopping bags from Gucci and Lord and Taylor.

"Kim, you need to see this three button suit." He spoke at me, unzipping the black Gucci garment bag, unmindful to my disconcerted demeanor.

I walked closer to the bed. Bags and white tissue paper were scattered lay on the bed and on the floor.

"What kind of store stays open until after midnight, Gbenga?" I felt the heat behind my eyes straightening out my eyelashes.

"We've been shooting dice most of the time. I got these earlier today." He smiled, pleased with himself as he pulled his new suit jacket over his shoulders and walked towards the mirror.

"Dice? You stayed out till day break shooting dice? Seriously? Your baby was up all day, then you come home while he is sleeping-for dice?" The words tasted funny coming out of my mouth.

"I got something for you baby." He walked over to the foot of the bed and handed me a large, brightly colored shopping bag with a bright yellow Medusa head on it.

Suddenly my shoes felt too tight, or maybe I just wanted to kick him, I don't know which; but I was stompin' angry. I made sure not to damage the Versace bag; my grandmother loves to recycle beautiful shopping bags when giving gifts, but I dumped the entire contents on the bed and rustled through the tissue paper. The first thing I saw was a black Versace purse; well, maybe I should call it a hand bag. It was a tiny clutch, with a gold Medusa head on it outlined in deco border filled with rhinestones. It had "bling." Wrapped in the tissue paper was a black sweater jacket trimmed in cream. It was thick and heavy, way too heavy for Houston, but good for winters back in Ohio.

It was double-breasted with gold buttons bearing the Versace logo. Lastly, I tipped open the shoe box. Ooh, the devil knows what you like. It was the sexiest pair of mules I had ever seen in my life. They were black satin mules with a 3 ½ inch heel, but the slide covered the top of your foot snuggly, with tiny gold Medusa heads in rows of two all the way up slightly past your ankle. I had never seen a pair of shoes like it. They were vicious! I slipped one on my foot. Cinderella couldn't have had better slippers.

"You like it?" Gbenga asked dropping his jeans to the floor to try on the pants to the suit.

"Yeah!" I responded, then looked up and caught some reality. Standing there looking at him in his $2,500 Prada suit jacket, with nothing on but a pair of briefs made me come down off my heels. "That is not the point, the point is you left here at 9:10 in the morning and it is now 1:00 the next day. I was up all night worried about you, and you were up all night, not thinking about us." I reached for the bag and noticed a receipt lying on the bed. Printed on the receipt was a total cost from Versace: $2,160. "And you spent how much?" I put the shoes back in the box.

"I'm taking you out tomorrow night, so I wanted to buy you something to wear," he remarked as he gestured toward the jacket.

"Out?" I smirked.

"Yeah, dinner at Papas Steak House, maybe to that new club on Richmond, and we can come home." He came over behind me and started kissing on my neck and pressing his body against me. I could feel he was hard. Funny that just the mention of good food, dancing and good dick can get you sidetracked.

"That sounds good, but I already have clothes in the closet I have never worn. You didn't need to go and spend this much money." I closed my eyes. He hadn't been so close to me, initiating anything, since we moved here.

"Well then, just put these in the closet for when you need them. My queen needs nice things." He backed off and walked away, taking his suit pants off the covered hanger and trying them on.

I always did like seeing a man in a pair of tailored pants.

*****

We went back and forth for months. We went to dinner or lunch at least twice a month, but we never ate together at the dinner table as a family. He would normally come in late, and he spent more weekends out of town on "business." Neglect was not making things better, no matter how elaborate he made the reception when he came home. Malcolm and I would play in the yard or go to the park; sometimes we would even make it to story time at the bookstore. Occasionally I would get to a spa to get a massage, but it all felt very empty. I bought lingerie from La Perla several times and wore it around the house hoping to get his attention, but it only caught me a cold.

"I want to go to Columbus." I lay on the bed still, as he crawled under the covers after two in the morning.

"I'm sorry, I was trying not to wake you," he whispered, timidly pulling the covers over my shoulders.

I turned my face to him, smelling a hint of Remy Martin. "A woman can hear your thoughts, let alone your footsteps," I thought to myself.

"Is everyone all right?" He moved freely, now that he knew I was awake.

"Everyone in Columbus is good. It's me that's not o.k." I tucked some of the sheet between us.

"Maybe we can talk about it tomorrow."

"I don't want to talk about it tomorrow. I may be gone tomorrow. I want to talk about it tonight."

"It's late."

I rolled over ranting in the dark. "Nice of you to notice. Doesn't that Rolex watch you wear tell time?" I searched hard in the dark of the night to see the whites of his eyes, but I could only see a glimmer of reflection. "We sit here all day, and where are you?"

"I am out hustlin' making money, trying to build for us."

"But you don't work a regular job." I wanted to say a real job, but I knew better. "What good is building when you lose the people you want to share it with? I just want you to be here and not miss your son's life. We're in the same house now and I am still showing you his greatest moments in pictures. I keep your other children on weekends and you're not even here when they are cussing, calling me a bitch and tellin' me I'm not their mama. I am trying, but I can do bad all by myself."

"Oh, you're not doing bad, designer clothes, a house full of furniture from Roche Bobois, limited edition paintings from William Tolliver and Richmond Barthe. Last month I gave you money for decorating! The house looks great. What else do you want?"

"I want you, I want us! I don't need to own any more things which could end up owning me. I want my son to know his Daddy is not an ass, because that is the only part he sees of you when you are leaving the house. I have clothes for going out and no one takes me out anywhere to wear them. I want you to tell me I am beautiful. I'd like you to touch my breasts and not look at them as feeding apparatuses constructed only for maternal responsibilities. I want to eat food that has not gotten cold because I wanted to wait and eat with my husband. Have you even stopped long enough to see what color I painted the kitchen? I don't need any of this stuff. As a matter of fact, you don't have to buy me another thing. I am going crazy sitting here all day. I don't even like soap operas. I have enough drama! I want to go back to work."

"What do you want to work for? Who will watch Malcolm?" his voice carried as he left the room.

"You are spending more and more time away from this house. I worry, I pray. For God's sake Gbenga, you could get popped. Someone could snitch on you. You are too comfortable hustlin'."

"I'm not out slangin' on corners, Kim."

"No, I know it, but just because your style of living has changed, the risk is just as high. If anything happens to you, none of your boys are going to help us. The ones working for you would plot to get what you've got, if they could get the opportunity, and every last Igbo in your clique wants to be the "big oga" in the village, so they are competing with you to see who can send the most money to Nigeria."

"Nothing is going to happen, and if it did, you and Malcolm would be fine."

"I'm not sure I can do this anymore." My voice cracked from frustration.

My nights seemed very cold in Houston. Gbenga and I hadn't slept together in more than seven months. Malcolm was going to a private school, and I got a position at a television station during the week selling advertising. It felt nice being out of the house, in the land of the "big people" having adult conversations about current events and not current cartoons. Sliding into a smart pair of heels and a business suit improved my posture from months of horsey rides and baths in the ball pit at the pizza place with Malcolm. My job description itself was dull, but I had a small opportunity for creativity. The pay was fair, the health insurance great, but the benefit was the recognition and reward for my hard work. That was what kept me going to work.

I had been a domestic administrator for some time and there had been no appreciation for what I was doing. Hours spent on dinner, and I would watch the steam disappear and the candles burn cold. A clothes hamper with no purpose would sit in the corner of the master bedroom as t-shirts and jeans lay on the floor, trailing into the bathroom. What really got me though, was the selective servitude: coming home with friends, unannounced, walking in the door smelling the food, serving himself and all of his friends without saying as much as a "hello," and not leaving a spoonful of food for me.

So I felt constantly passed over. But at the station I had my first review and received a small raise. It was an accomplishment of sorts, yet a storm was brewing at home.

"Who was that guy who held the elevator for you this morning?"

I noticed a muscle jumping along his jaw. "I don't know."

"That guy. He was kind of stocky, brown skin, suit and tie. Who was he?"

"I have no idea. Where were you when you saw him?"

"I was in the parking lot, and you know who I am talking about because you spoke to him."

I could feel my back pushing further into the cushions on the couch, so I got up. "Oh, that was probably Mr. Keenan, my Supervisor. We work on the same floor."

"Oh, so that's the man who gave you a raise?" Gbenga asked as he stood up, walking in my direction.

"No. He gave me a recommendation, but Mr. Ellis gave me a raise." I knew where this conversation was going. Gbenga had gotten an idea in his head and I was going to have to wait out the storm.

"So what kinds of things did you have to do for this raise?" he asked, his words spilling like chocolate syrup.

"Nothing, Gbenga, just doing my job, that's all. Please, I am going to bed." I walked out of the room, closed the door to Malcolm's room and went to the bedroom.

I was slipping my shirt off over my head when I felt the thrust of a hand pulling me towards the floor. My shirt swung over me and landed beside the bed. My temperature shot up, and my heart raced. My body hadn't had a release in more than six months, but this wasn't the way I yearned to be taken. This was shocking, and who doesn't like a spontaneous, rip-off -your stockings, grab-the-back-of-your-hair "do me" once in awhile? No, this was cold, an invasion by a familiar face. He pushed himself inside of me. I was bone dry. It was burning with every thrust. I couldn't even close my eyes. I stared looking at him, anger in his face so old, breathing heavy, grunting, moaning until he shuddered, face tense, ejaculating inside of me. I jerked as he held my shoulders down, digging them into the carpet, now glaring at me. I didn't make a sound. A tear dropped back from my eye. His touch and his dick, two elements that could make me scream in ectasy, feeling desire and passion, made me shrink in aching defeat. He rolled off and slept, his arm possessively draped over my waist. I sprung up, remembering I had stopped my birth control pills a long time ago. I went to the kitchen and grabbed a cold bottle of water. I tore through the linen closet looking for a disposable douche. I twisted off the plastic seal, emptied it and filled it with the ice cold spring water. I put the nozzle inside of me and squeezed streams of freezing cold water until the bottle gave way and was empty. My body tensed; I felt nauseated. I wanted to wash all traces of this off of me. I got in the shower, scrubbing with the loofa until the drops of water burned my skin. Wrapping up in a terry cloth bathrobe, I opened the door to Malcolm's room. He was sleeping so sound, his bottom lip quivering as I covered him tightly in his covers and kissed his head.

I continued to go to work, but my phone never stopped ringing. Gbenga's calls grew more and more frequent until it became a running joke with my colleagues. Gbenga didn't find the laughs funny at all. He came up to my job one day during lunch. I was sitting with Mr. Keenan and Tracy Parker, a friend from my office. He didn't come in, he just sat outside in the parking lot, where I could see him from the cafeteria window. I finished eating and went outside. He yelled and accused, pointing his finger in my face as I stood aware that people were watching. Insult after insult tore at me until I gathered every broken piece of myself and buttoned up my suit jacket so they wouldn't fall out, and he slithered away. I got inside the building to find Mr. Keenan standing in the atrium, carrying my cranberry juice and turkey sandwich. He handed them to me and didn't say a word, he didn't have to. I grabbed the plate. He held my fingers, released them and walked away. I knew I wanted more that day, more from a man, more from a relationship, more out of myself. I finished out my workday making quite a few sales. I arrived at Malcolm's school in time to see him tumbling during his gymnastics class and then we headed home.

Malcolm and I sat on the floor eating rice and stew. The rice would have ended up there anyway, so I saved myself a step. When Malcolm finished, he told me all about his day, his teacher, and how his friend Forest ate a bug.

Night crept in and made the sky an inky black. I couldn't sleep, so I lay in bed thinking about Malcolm. Every day he takes in all that's around him. I remember driving up and down roads I didn't know with directions given to me by a man at a filling station who barely spoke good English, looking at school after school, until I was satisfied with one I thought would challenge and nurture his mind. I wanted him to feel comfortable with strangers in the classroom, but I closed my eyes to the imbalance, which we had in our house. My jumbled thoughts were interrupted by the agile movements of light across the ceiling descending to intensify on the wall beside me. As I started out of bed, the lights vanished and I heard the front door being opened. I plucked my legs back into bed when I heard humming through the hallway.

"Kim! Kim! Kim, there's nothing to eat. Come help me find something to eat." Gbenga's voice echoed through the house, weaving through every thread in my sheets, making it uncomfortable to stay in bed. I closed my eyes, but he kept calling, and like crumbs on the sheets scratching against my skin. I had to get out of bed to find a solution.

The light stung my eyes, but I could see cabinet doors hanging open. "I put all of the food away in the refrigerator. Just open the containers and put some in the microwave." He looked as if I were speaking a foreign language. "I'm going to bed."

He snatched the back of my shirt, seams ripping under my arms. I lost my balance and fell against the counter, my back scraping skin on my way down. "Gbenga, it's two a.m. I couldn't leave the food out on the stove. Just warm it up." No sooner had I closed my mouth on the last syllable than fury gaped it open. Two quick punches followed, with a flat hard slapping sound, and the floor came to meet my face. I caught my breath with a wet choke and spit freeing some air. My eye was watering and pulsating, the bridge of my nose was numb, and my cheekbone pulsed with fire. My bare feet were like skates on the tile fumbling to gain ground.

"Oh, you can get up and run to work when they call, but you can't take care of me." He talked leaning with one hand on the stove. His voice echoed, or my ears were ringing, I'm not sure which. I ran to reach for the phone, my fingers shaking as I called my grandparents' house.

"Hello. Hello?" My grandfather's voice became solemn. "Love bugs, is that you?" I'm sure he was looking at the caller i.d.

I couldn't grab my voice. It was concealed in my chest, pushed out on strained pockets of breath. "Gran…Gben..hit…me."

"What! What? I can't understand you. He hit you! Hang up. I am calling the police there."

The phone went dead as I was still talking. Gbenga's open hand approached me, I steadied myself on the couch, jerking my leg back to nail him in the balls. A fury of movement erupted, an entanglement of arms against flesh until I felt the receiver of the phone lash against my brow bone and my temple. My face was ablaze. A knot, round and warm to the touch formed over my eye, both eyes swollen and blue beneath my brown skin, his hand grabbing me by the hair, stretching my neck back so I could face him.

"Go move in with your supervisor! You wanna jump up when they call? Get your shit and go, bitch! I am not going to be put second. Just go!" His voice was thunderous, and most of his energy spent, but a creek of the door cut through it all. Malcolm had been listening.

"I'm not going anywhere, Gbenga. You are! The police are on their way." I talked loud, palms on the floor and head hung, hoping to give more elasticity to the skin on my puffed-up face.

Gbenga grabbed his keys and tore out the door.

"Who's the bitch?" I cried out to an audience of myself waving my bold and silent middle finger. Malcolm was still standing in the doorway. I went to him, arms open, but he turned inside the room, closing the door and sliding his back up against it so I couldn't get in. "I'm sorry baby, open the door. It's all right, no more fighting."

There was a knock at the door. I couldn't make out the figure through the peephole, my left eye was completely swollen shut. I pulled back the sheer curtain on the side window by the door and saw two policemen standing on the porch. I opened the door.

"He's gone," I said, opening the door to allow them to come inside.

"What happened, ma'am?" The officer asked, looking over my shoulder and scanning the room.

I turned up my lip, raw, stinging as it slipped across my teeth. "He hit me."

"Is he still here ma'am?" asking as he walked in the living room.

"No, he isn't here. He left, and I am leaving. I just want to get my things."

"How long will it take you to get your things ma'am?" The officer walked into the hallway, noticing a moving shadow beneath the crack in the door. He pressed up against the door, his hand moving towards his revolver.

Knock, knock, knock

"I'm just playing, Mommy."

The officer's hand relaxed and I moved passed him to open the bedroom door.

"Would you like to press charges?"

"I would like to leave and not lay eyes on him again. Pressing charges means going through the motions and if I don't show up for court I will have to deal with the repercussions of calling the police later. NO THANK YOU!"

"I see this all of the time," pleaded the officer. "You don't see all that I see. I am telling you- press charges while you are still here to do so."

I touched my baby's face and went to his closet to get some of his clothes. "That's just it, officer; I'm not going to be here. And I don't want to come back to Houston just to go to court, and who is to say the judge I meet sees things from that perspective?"

"Well, ma'am, we can't stay here if you are not pressing charges, so I suggest you get what you can and go."

Before the officer left he snapped a picture and held it in his hand. I watched as the dull gray coating in the center of the bright white frame slithered to form silhouettes and glossy outlines. I turned to close the door right as I got a glimpse of the puffed-up image that lay beneath. I looked around the house at mementos and necessary items I needed to pack and take with me. My eyes only kept coming back to Malcolm. I remembered there were clothes I had been washing. There were panties and t-shirts in the washer. I usually hang them to dry, but I didn't have the time to get them. I opened the dryer only to find Gbenga's shirts and a few socks. Shirts I would be spraying to iron, had I been staying, ironing perfect creases on each sleeve. I tossed them all into a basket one after the other until some toppled onto the floor. I turned the dial on the dryer to air dry, moved the clothes, and pushed the button.

Malcolm sat in the middle of a pile of action figures and matchbox cars, clutching a tiny suitcase with his "most valuables" on his lap. I couldn't help but smile at the sight of it all. I grabbed all of my bags and my keys and opened the door. "Damn!" I dropped my bags on the walkway, eyes blurred from water that could not fall to tears from the swelling that hid my eyelashes. My damn BMW was gone, and in its place was Gbenga's Range Rover, which I didn't have a key for. I fell to my knees, head bowed, still holding two duffle bags in my hands. "Father, deliver me, I am weak, deliver me." At that moment a light reflected off the chrome on the side of the Range Rover. I snapped up, throwing one of the duffle bags into the bushes in front of the house. I walked backwards up the walkway tripping into the front door, my heart racing and my thoughts scattered. I put the other bags in Malcolm's closet and closed the door. The beams from the headlights inched past the driveway and the car they belonged to came into clear view. It was not my car. Grabbing a bag of black-eyed peas from the freezer, funny enough, I sat on the couch shuddering as the cold package rested on my face. Malcolm climbed up on my lap, inquisitive mini fingers navigating the swells around my eyes as if I were wearing a rubber mask. I walked with him into his room, wishing the dark would hide my frailties. We slept until I heard the door.

Gbenga came in not saying a word. I lay in the bed letting time pass the usual countdown to his explosions. He was asleep, but I knew walking past him unnoticed wouldn't be possible once I opened the door. I grabbed the keys to the car on the table in front of him. The rattling woke him up, but he didn't move his position on the couch. He mumbled a few words and asked me where I was going. I told him I was leaving and taking Malcolm with me. He still didn't move. I didn't stop. I kept collecting and grabbing until my bag was full. I grabbed the bag from Malcolm's closet and walked out the door, snatching the sack from behind the bushes. I popped the trunk open and threw the bags inside. When I came in, Gbenga sat watching television. He looked over at me then back at the television. "Where do you think you're going?" His words were muffled and then trailed off.

I approached Malcolm's door. Not a sound. The silence gave me a boost of assurance, so I lifted Malcolm and carried him out the door and to the car, closing the door behind me.

It was Christmas Eve and we drove into the night. Nearly eight hours and what seemed like millions of dashes left behind in the middle of the interstate when we reached Texarkana and Malcolm awoke. Dawn had already broken open with rays of coral sunshine when he looked at the landscape on the fringes of the road. "Where are we, Mom?"

"We're near Arkansas."

"Where are we going?"

"We're going to Grandma and Grandpa's for Christmas."

A large billboard in the near distance publicized McDonalds at the next exit. I saw him read intently until the very moment we passed it. "I need to use the bathroom, can we stop?"

"How about we stop at the McDonald's up the way? The sign back there said they had a play area." He smiled and I grinned as we made our way off the freeway.

Shoes off and stomachs full of salty french fries, we were ready to hit the road again. Two hours into the drive the billows of white marshmallow clouds thinned out to a gray haze. The weather was changing as quickly as we were riding with it. We laughed and sang as I put more and more distance between us and the madness back in Houston.

Snowflakes were silently falling against the windshield, each one taking its own beautiful shape then disappearing against the glass. The sky seemed to be void and grieving, but in its sorrow intricate flakes of splendor emerged to be carried by the winds. I glanced over at Malcolm's sweet face. He was the marvel amidst a troubled backdrop. Several choruses of "Jingle Bells" later, we drove more than sixteen hours, drunk more than five bottles of orange soda, and chewed countless sticks of chewing gum, and at last, turning into Wellington Ridge.

We arrived on Pine Valley Road. The house was twinkling with icicles and the Christmas tree glistened through the cream sheers in the living room. This is home base, the time-out zone, the space that brings me back to me. I pushed the car door as the cold air bit my face and slashed through my clothes. Malcolm sat up, startled from the chill or the close of the car door. I opened the door and my Grandma Nellie stood with a sweet smile on her face. My cousin used to always say the house smelled like cornbread, and the sweet aroma enveloped my head and lightened my heart. She didn't have to say a word. She just took my puffy face in her hands and brought me close to kiss my forehead. "This is right where you need to be," she said, her smile returning.

A few days of rest and occupying myself to avoid phone calls, I was ready to think about my next tomorrows. I heard my grandfather asking Malcolm questions about the cartoon playing on the television. I stood and watched as Kazoo sat over top of Fred Flintstone thunking him on the head: "This is some kind of a mess you got yourself into now, Dumb Dumb."

So, I wondered, does putting someone down ever cause them to change? Is it everywhere? Grandma hummed "Love Lifted Me" while folding laundry in the front room. I was comforted, but not comfortable. There was consolation that Gbenga and I were not in the same city. My concerns of running into him were hardly an issue- Gbenga never did snow with any grace at all. But the last time I was here, I wasn't Kim-single mother. I was Kim, successful restaurant owner, able to leap over lunch crowds and piled high dishes in four-inch stilettos and a smile. The question kept itching at me: What went wrong?

"Hey baby, why don't you get out of that dark room and get out for a while?" Grandma posed, brushing my hair from my face.

"Have you seen what I look like? It doesn't come close to what I feel like. I have made a mess out of my life."

"Your messes will often end up being a message. You can use them as stumbling blocks or you can use them as stepping stones," Grandma smiled, revealing her long soft chin. "Ten percent of life is what happens to you, the other ninety percent is what you make out of what happened."

If I had to write my jobs in order of importance on a resume, mother would be at the very top. I got jazzed with every opportunity to observe or deliver life's lessons for Malcolm. Whether through hugs, bed time stories, at the dinner table, playing in the house, or upside his head, he deserved my full attention and I tried to be present when it was his time. Every yesterday was once a tomorrow and I only prayed to teach him about the strength he came from so he could take it along with him.

I sat in the chair watching and reflecting as my father engaged with Malcolm as though it were a highlight on the Discovery Channel. It was my dad who seemed curious and almost uncomfortable with the interaction.

"Hey man, whatcha doin?" he asked loudly, as Malcolm rolled his cars across the tile floor in the kitchen. "You know who I am?" Malcolm turned with a vacant expression. "I'm your Grandpa, your Grand-pa!"

"Daddy, I think he remembers who you are. It's just been a long time, that's all, but he understands just fine," I whispered, holding Malcolm's hand and leading him to his grandpa. "Baby, give Papa Ricky a hug and show him how fast you can make your cars go."

Malcolm scooped all of his cars in his arms, handed one to his grandpa and walked towards the farthest end of the tile where it met the carpet. "Come on, Papa Ricky, you gotta bring your car to the race track, back here." My dad looked at me, almost surprised at Malcolm's acceptance. I smiled with understanding, signaling with a raise of my eyebrows: don't waste time thinking you don't know how to be the best Grandpa, just spend time being his Grandpa.

*****

The dad that raised me was amazing. He was tall and thin, dark, short hair, with German features, quirky ears, and a voice for talk radio. Other than the obvious color difference signaling we weren't blood related, he treated me just like his daughter and gave me fond memories of camping trips, canoe rides, nature walks and dances to jazz music while standing on his toes. He came to all of my sporting events when I was growing up and understood adoption wasn't a substitute for either of us, but a bonus. He would say: "I am proud that you picked me to be your daddy." It takes a special man to love and provide for someone else's child as his own. He tried to be my bridge and my safety net in an environment where I wasn't equipped to separate myself from the stereotypes and bad racial jokes, and they weren't equipped to talk about the differences and the issues. For the most part I grew up with a father figure in the house, but there was always a nagging hurt inside of me that my real mom and dad were going on with their lives, not coming to see about me. Time had passed and I was grown. I didn't want to swap one set of memories for the possibilities of wishes. My mind moves through the sequence: the dad who gave me up and the one who was chosen for me. I don't want Malcolm to wonder who he is because he can't identify whose he is.

*****

"Love bugs, I want to talk to you for a minute," my Grandpa called.

"Sir."

"Kim, marriage takes work. Maybe it's best you don't have job for awhile. Stay home with Malcolm. If Gbenga can provide for your family comforts, don't nag him, let him provide."

"Grandpa, I know marriage takes work. I knew that going in. I asked him about going back to work. Why is this becoming my fault?" I felt myself shrinking into a tiny little girl.

"I am not saying it is your fault, I am saying be smart. Doesn't he give you money to pay the bills?"

"Yes sir."

"Well, then, ask him for a little more each month as an allowance and save that money up for you and your son."

"He asks me how much money I need to take care of the bills. He's never asked me to see the bills, because he trusts me to handle the money. There is going to be one time he does ask and I will have to explain. I don't want to have to back pedal. Why can't I just tell him I want to start a savings account? I didn't agree to marry with an exit strategy. Isn't that dishonest?"

"Do you think he is going to take care of you and Malcolm first? Is he providing you with security?"

I sat and paused to reflect. One thing I knew for sure about Gbenga was his generosity. Sometimes when I thought he wasn't paying the slightest attention, he would blow me away. I rarely had to ask for anything twice. I don't mean the: 'look at that handbag' or 'that bracelet would look good on me' type of ask, I always had a job, I could get those for myself. I'm talking about the time I casually mentioned my Grandma's broken watch. Four days later, she called to thank me for the beautiful watch shipped to her from Cartier. There was also the time a fellow Nigerian came to the house in tears, heavy with the pain of losing his father and not having enough money to bury him. This guy's sister was married into Gbenga's family, yet she and her brother constantly prayed for Gben's downfall. They turned their nose up at him because he sold drugs once upon a time, but they had no trouble spending his dirty money. Gbenga knew this, but he didn't hesitate to give the guy money so he could have a large burial ceremony for his father. The condition; he couldn't tell anyone where he got the money from. We heard about the pageantry of the burial back in Houston, but all Gbenga did was sit back on the phone, nod his head and smile. "I would say he was generous, openhanded, mmm-hmm, occasionally closefisted. He is a provider. But security is more than financial."

"Yes, love bugs, but no one is perfect."

"You're right Grandpa, no one is perfect. I know I am not perfect, and I'm not expecting him to be perfect. I just want someone who is going to love me in all my imperfections and recognize I love him in spite of his."

"He has admitted he was wrong and he wants to try and make it up to you."

"Grandpa, words are easy. I don't want to hear Gbenga's words on the phone that is why I haven't been taking his calls."

"I know. That is why I told him he should come here if he wants you back."

"I guess I will see when that time comes."

"He will be here tonight."

"Tonight? How do you know?" I got up from the chair.

"He has called almost every day since you have been here. I can tell he is sorry. He is crazy about you and Malcolm. Give him a chance. You know you love him."

"YOU are amazing!" raising my hands in frustration. "This man puts his hands on me and you invite him to the house."

"This man wants to be your husband. He's your son's father. He has made a mistake. We have all fallen short." He stands, eye brows raised, glancing at my father and grandmother in hopes of a co-signer.

I lower my eyes, wondering what the hell is a matter with him? Why does my grandfather still see me as a child? I have a child. "AMEN." I threw back the comment as I walked down the hallway. I left the door open and flung myself on the bed.

Later in the evening, I woke to the sound of Malcolm's laugh. I rolled out of the bed and stopped short at the bedroom door, my body stiffening, when I heard Gbenga's voice.

"I'm a good man."

"What makes you a good man Gbenga? Is it because your momma said so? Because your other children, who aren't in the house with you all of the time think so? Or maybe some hot in the pants little girl, who isn't around to clean up after you told you so? Most people can pretend some of the time. If you really want to know someone, spend a lot of time with them. Gbenga, a good man doesn't have to declare it. People declare it for him. A man's goodness is measured by what each person looking at him finds value in. Do you know what Kim finds value in?"

"Yes ma'am. Kim loves family, and I want to give her a family. I love her, my parents adore her, and my kids can't stop asking about her. My house is not a home without her. If she will have me back I want to take her and Malcolm home."

"Can we go home?"

I shrugged. "I don't know," I answered, locking eyes with Gbenga the entire time.

Gbenga walked towards me slowly and took a deep breath. "Tell me what to do to make this right."

"I don't have any magic answers. I just know I can't love you when I want to run away from you."

"I wish I could take it back. But I can't. All I can do now is take time showing you how much I cherish you," he softly reached for my fingers, then my hand, wrapping my entire body into his. Malcolm's arms fastened like a vice, squeezing us together like a peanut butter and jelly sandwich. I exhaled, slowly closing my eyes, releasing myself into the moment.

"I don't want to lose you. Find it in your heart to forgive me Kim. We have a son. We're going to have some kind of relationship for him regardless, but give me a chance to give you the relationship you want starting today."

"O.k," I responded, squeezing him closer. "We will give it a fresh start." I walked to the room to pack our bags.

"Gbenga, this is my grandbaby's house. She will always have a place to stay and bring my great grandbaby with her. She is loved and safe here. Don't think for one moment we will not come and get them if they are being mistreated. And God help you if I find out you have put your hands on her again." She rose out of the dining room chair, crumbs from her cornbread falling off her apron to the floor. "You can't hide anything from Him, and He always knows where to find you." She turned her glare away from him, and turned to look at me.

"Yes, ma'am," Gbenga responded, picking up our bags. "I understand."

"Gbenga, don't let me down."

Grandma's words sunk deeply in my heart. Many people say they love God, but they don't love people. Grandma found God in everyone. In seventy eight years I never heard her say; "You should listen to me because I am older and wiser." She never had to stomp or raise her voice to get me, or anyone else to listen. It had nothing to do with her age or her position; it had to everything to do with her willingness to be obedient to God. Because I knew no matter how old you are, if you aren't obedient, you will have consequences too.

There is a part of me that wants to stay away from Gbenga, a section that hears all of the warnings and replays countless scenes from television dramas. I hear the vows in sickness, til death do us…But then, there is another part, a place deep inside of me, beneath my heart, that wants to love and yearns to beat the curse that mocks over and over declaring I can't be loved, or at least not enough to be kept. So I went, and the moment was picturesque: father, mother, and little boy, all holding hands, waving goodbye on the quest for a renewed love. It was an illusion, not a dream, one that would blur my eyes and alter my vision.

*****

Back in Houston in my own house, it was easy for us to settle back into our old routine. Malcolm trotted into his room to find all of his old toys. It had been a few months, but he knew exactly where his action figures had been stored. He went to his drawer and pulled out his Batman pajamas with the detachable cape, pulled the pj shirt over his tiny head and whisked out of the room to play on the back porch. The refrigerator was full of half-open, half-eaten carry- out and a liter of flat soda. I pulled up the trash can and started dumping things in. Gbenga came behind me wrapping his arms around my waist. "It feels so good to have my family home. I am going to do better at making you happy. We are going to be a closer family. We don't have to have a fuss of a wedding. My family is out of the country; your family is out of the state. Let's go make this official."

"Holy matrimony?" I whispered, turning to look in his face.

"Holy matrimony."

Duct Tape

Stop and listen..................

A late- night phone call altered my job search. There was to be a burial in Nigeria and I would have to go to represent Gbenga. I was grieved that I was going to his grandmother's funeral, the very sweet frail woman with brown crepe-paper skin I had met over a year ago. I remembered during my last visit, her husband offered me a kola nut while she held Malcolm, the first great-grandchild she could touch, on her lap, with tears streaming down her thin-textured face. Gbenga was noticeably shaken, speaking Igbo in very low tones, offering sympathy and condolence over the phone. He hadn't seen her in nearly nineteen years. He was aching and our relationship was hurting. I didn't know how to console him. I had almost forgotten he had feelings. How could he hit me, bruise me, and break me, and have feelings? I wanted to hold him, but was not ready to feel his touch, the stroke with the ability to slay you and bring you back to life.

For weeks Gbenga stayed in the house meditating over melancholy tunes and meticulously arranging his CD collection according to genre and alphabetical by artist.

"I thought I had more time to see her again."

"Tomorrow is not promised." I turned to face him, noticing the pain that shattered the deep brown of his eyes, and I knew he was hurting and the comfort he needed from me was more immediate than the assurances I needed from him. I took a breath and swallowed, holding on enough to kiss him.

Swiftly Gbenga took me in his arms, carrying me down the hallway. He tip toed past Malcolm's door to see if he had woken from his nap. He lowered me gently on the bed, so cautiously not one down feather in the comforter moved. He started by kissing my finger tips, pausing to suck lightly on my wedding ring finger, ending by trailing his tongue across every line in the palm of my hand. Slowly he unbuttoned my blouse running his hand under the nylon straps of my bra so he could massage both of my breasts at the same time, paying close attention as he rolled my nipples between his fingers. I rubbed the back of his neck, bringing his mouth closer to my breasts. He licked a trail with his tongue from my nipples down to my belly button, stopping to flick his tongue in it. My stomach tickled as I felt the vibration of his heavy breathing drying his saliva from my skin. My bruises had since faded, but he moved very cautiously, tracing every curve with the warm softness of his tongue. Every hair follicle on my body became a heightened receptor.

Closing my eyes and feeling strong and melted at the same time, the moment became slippery. I gripped, "I'm sorry. I am so blessed to have you." He sank, pulling me closer.

"I'm here." I softened.

"I love you." He exploded.

"Love me." I released, I shivered. He exhaled.

*****

I gathered my luggage for the trip home to the village packing extras for the occasion: fine jewelry for Mama, nice skirt suits for my sisters accessorized with beautiful large-brimmed church hats. The gifts were bulky, so I packed my own clothes in with Malcolm's things. Gbenga handed me $15,000 and a letter to give his mother. He always had a natural tendency to care for people, but where expressing was difficult for him, he threw money at it.

Back again in Nigeria we stayed in Lagos with my brothers, but by morning we would be traveling to the East. That evening, Ufoma, Gbenga's middle sister, came to me with a bowl of nsala soup, shortbread for Malcolm, and a list of items needed for the burial. I wanted to get confirmation from Gbenga about some of the items on the list, but there would be no time to do so. Taking a car across I.B.B. Bridge to the marina to make an international call at Nitel would take up time and the phones at Papa's house in the village were not reliable. I took the list and read each item: silk blue ashoke, cream Five-diamond lace and Dutch Wax, each with people's names beside them. I looked at the items across from my name. "What is this?"

Ufoma looked at me and smiled, "Mama Chibu, we all need to be in uniform for the burial. Only Mama will have different lace."

"You mean we will all be dressed alike?" The visual made me laugh. "How will we have time to make these things?"

"I will buy them first thing in the morning near Balogun market before we travel and we will make them in the East after getting everyone's measurements."

"I only want to go and see about Mama and then she can tell me what I need to do." I said, still tickled at the site of a parade of us all dressed in the same cloth.

"But the selection of lace in Lagos will be nicer than what we may find in Enugu."

I looked in her face. I had been to a wedding in Nigeria before and I knew that weddings and funerals are a show of pageantry, an opportunity to show the "who's who" of the village. An unlikely place for someone from my culture to think of finding a companion, but in Nigeria it gives suitors an opportunity to size up a potential mate and their family by what was on display. And true enough, Lagosians take their appearance very seriously. People are always neat and presentable, because in Lagos it is believed you have to. Appearance matters to me, but Nigerians- and Lagosians in particular- are the most status- and style-conscious people I have ever been around. There are over fifteen million people, so they believe you have to stand out. Sometimes standing out is not enough. Ufoma wanted to be sure we would stop traffic. I asked her the cost of the lace and the ashoke' and calculated the conversion from naira to dollars times five. I called Chike and asked him if he could exchange one hundred dollars for me into naira and counted out nine hundred dollars to give Ufoma.

The sun rested patiently against the window as I woke to the Lagos heat. The air conditioner must have stopped when NEPA; the Nigerian Electric Power Authority, took light during the night. My body was sticky and Malcolm had tiny bumps on his cheeks where his face wedged against my sweaty arm. I woke to take a shower, the cool water soothing my skin and shaking my jet lag. Ufoma tapped at the door with a tray of breakfast in her hand.

"Good morning, Mama Chibu."

"Good morning." The title takes some getting used to. "When are we leaving?"

"Two hours time," she says, hoisting Malcolm to her back. "I will bathe him. Where are his clothes?"

I handed her his clothes and sat on the bed. The sun and smell of sweet bougainvillea danced through the window sheers. I thought for a moment about the splendor of all the simple things in Nigeria. The blooming tropical flowers made beautiful for their own sake, inviting adoration simply because they are. The possibilities and potential were around every corner. Lagos was like a VCR with the time not set. It is contemporary, not the latest in technology, capable of sending bold sound and millions of bursts of color charging into view, but where time is just standing still, flashing as a reminder over and over for you to take notice. Everyone sees the problem. They talk about it, they point at it, but no one is stopping to fix it.

The tops of the tall palms became woven together like a basket and swallowed the sun. Many hours and several police checkpoints later, we arrived in the village. Malcolm was drained, but no one let his feet touch the ground. As big as he was, he dangled from one pair of hands to the next. I came down from the car, eyes burning from the red dust and hot dry sun. My father-in-law stood dressed in a white t-shirt and wrapper looking over from the balcony. "Welcome, welcome!" he bellowed, his smile beaming, competing with the setting sun. Papa waved his hands high above his head like a Pentecostal praise dancer. His burgeoning belly, a 'dunlap' that undermined the hint of his past glory on a soccer pitch, marred his physique. Mama rose and walked slowly from beneath the whirl of the ceiling fan. She tightened her patterned scarlet wrapper around her waist and reached out for Malcolm, "Chibu, bia, nun o!" She palmed his chin beneath the soft fat of his cheek and smiled. I know she was in pain at the loss of her mother, but she grinned over her grandson. She was both tender and tough, stocky build with flawless black walnut skin and dimples that danced with her smile. My heart felt light knowing that our long journey helped to soothe her loss.

The next day it was seven o'clock in the morning when the tailor and the hair stylist came by. My eyes were still heavy and my throat was dry when I came out of the room. I walked to the bathroom with my towel and toothbrush in hand when I was greeted by a voice coming from the parlor. "My wife!" The voice was audacious, as a small older woman wearing a buba made of bright green jacquard came down the hallway, smiling carrying a large white chicken by its feet.

"Good morning, ma." I said with a small curtsy. She smiled, holding a small chewing stick between her teeth. I was never interested in meeting what I was about to eat, so I made my way to the bathroom and closed the door.

Water gurgled through the water heater above the bathtub, making its way down the pipes as a tiny waterfall escaping the faucet. I stepped into the tub; icy chills went throughout my body. "Damn, no light!"

I quickly rubbed some soap on the sponge, squeezing the excess water before it chilled my skin. I made my way down the hallway, the fisk, fisk of my flip flops following me as I made my way down the hallway. I rubbed my skin with coconut oil while it was still damp and pulled a crisp linen dress over my head. The hairdresser waited for me on the veranda beneath the ceiling fan. A tall stool and a wicker chair were placed in the sun. We sat down as she asked me the length I would like my braids.

The flat rattail comb, like a tiny finger into my scalp, divided my hair into sections like a map, pulling out tension from my temples. It felt somewhat pleasant, but after several hours my hair was so taught I could barely blink.

My mother-in-law came out to meet me on the porch; her dark-skinned bare feet were covered with saffron soil where she had been overseeing the cooking in the back. Women watched over large iron pots and pounded yams in wooden mortars with large sticks as tall as me. I admired her so much.

"Mama Chibu, you look hungry, come sit and eat with me" she called.

I sat beside her on the chair. I sighed, quietly listening to her. Momma's voice rustled like silk, humming spiritual, yet native, soft and husky tones spilling into my eardrums.

"What is troubling you my daughter? Your heart and head have seemed heavy since you arrived."

I hesitated to speak. "Mama, Gbenga has been hitting me. If we hadn't received the news from Nigeria, I don't think he and I would still be together. His anger is too much. I don't know that person he becomes. I look into his eyes and try to find him, but all I see are two lobes a peculiar shade of ice. I love him from my skin to my soul, but I can't reach him. Did Papa ever hit you?" I sat waiting for a response, an excuse, some shade of gray I could stick on this problem like duct tape either to hold my love in or attach like a banner over my heart.

Her eyes held a story as she looked at me, holding my hand and resting deeply in her chair. "You can live with anything if you have the things with you which you can't live without."

I sat beside her, as she continued to hold my hand thinking about what she said.

The rainy season had swallowed up the landscape, each tire muddled over tiny breaks in the road. We passed Oraifite junction where small knots of people were gathering to watch the chaos displayed by the local militia task force, the Bakassi boys. Their efforts to keep Anambra safe of armed robbers were barbaric forms of jungle justice that had gotten out of hand. A huge cloud of black smoke mixed with a stench that burned my nostrils seeped through the vents in the car. Ufoma quickly turned to Malcolm and masked his face in her lap as we maneuvered by. Peeking through the gaps of people I could see a severed bloody torso partially charred to a horrid blackness propped in the center of a tire, both blazing with fire. The smell was so thick; musky burnt liver, interlocked with metallic sulfur, I could nearly taste it. My mouth began to water immediately as I felt my stomach locking. We drove carefully as I fastened my seat belt. As we cleared past the people, I hastily opened the door leaving chunks of my morning breakfast along the road.

The small market at the junction where I remember buying bananas was empty, mats folded in respect for the burial. We arrived at the compound in Amichi. Tents were being set up in the sun as a multitude of people gathered to deliver cartons of beer, crates of soft drinks and trays of local biscuits. We made it through the crowd to greet Gbenga's Uncle Sammy seated at the head table. Papa walked proudly, his red cap adorned with one feather propped lightly on his head, as he pulled a large cow behind him as a gift of dedication. The rest of the family followed, the girls each carrying large white hens by the legs, while I carried a small piece of rope to symbolize the offering of a goat. The celebration continued with electrifying dances performed in colorful synchronization by members representing each in-law's family. The drums, praise singers and metal percussion continued in hypnotizing rhythms while I danced beside Momma and the other women from the village. Spectators showed their approval by spraying money around us until piles of dusty naira notes covered the ground. Malcolm flitted around our legs like a tiny gnat, placing as much as his tiny hands could carry into a bag. The day and pageantry rolled on and it felt much more like a party that the somber funerals I was used to. No black, no veils; only dancing, drinking and drums.

My body had longed stopped, but my stomach continued to roll over itself pushing saliva into my mouth and barricade behind my lips. Then, finally my stomach heaved and vomit propelled down towards the ground. My nose and throat were burning and my head was light with a familiar but unsettling feeling. Papa Ndili balanced my arm as he lowered me to sit in the chair. "Mama Chibu, please come out of the sun," he guided in an urgent whisper. I nodded in response as Ufoma removed the gele from my head.

I watched the rest of the procession from the sidelines having no taste to eat anything for the rest of the night. My sisters doted over Malcolm, feeding and playing with him, while fighting back their own tears of sorrow during the burial. As the sun tipped to the west, turning gaps of sky like fall foliage, we gathered into our cars for the caravan back to the East.

Awakened by the roosters call, I gingerly got out of bed careful not to rouse Malcolm. I left the bedroom to walk out on the balcony. The air is warm and the trees on the hills look painted against the sky. Suddenly, my stomach is twisting followed by an ice cold jolt up the base of my spine. I felt my lips wet and part, but I didn't vomit. I felt hungry, but thinking about what I wanted turned my stomach more. This queasiness was unsettling, but familiar. I ran back everything I had eaten since I arrived in the village. My family was very strict about not allowing Malcolm and me to eat food while visiting with neighbors. The screens on all of the windows in our room were intact and Ufoma sprayed as a precaution before we slept. I have only been drinking bottled water. My period seldom gave me cramps, but never made me—"Oh!" I laughed inside of myself and dropped to my knees. "I guess your time is best God."

I heard Momma's bare feet thump mildly as she entered to the concrete balcony floor. Mike, the house boy followed. The spoon jingled against the tea set as he placed the tray next to the end table. "Ibola chi my daughter," she greeted. "Come sit by me and have some tea."

"Thank you. Daalu Momma, but my stomach is not feeling very

well." I replied, sitting on the edge of the chair.

"Ay wo," she sympathized. "Michael, boil some ginger and bring me the water," she instructed, flipping her wrists to signal the urgency. "Maybe it's malaria," she deliberated, touching my forehead with the pads of her fingers. "I can send for Fansidar."

"Mba! No," I shook my head. "No Fansidar. It's not malaria." The sing song in my voice raised Momma's suspicion. The feathery touch of her palm slid off my forehead swiftly clapping her other hand like a magnetic attraction.

"Hey!" Momma danced, chuckles slipping between the spaces in her teeth.

I sat down in the thumping jubilation, not aware of all the words spoken until Malcolm entered dragging his bath towel behind him. They all calmed in his presence long enough to speak to him in English.

"Good morning Chibu, big brother," Ufoma called gleefully. "Mommy is going to have another baby."

Papa didn't try to hide his glee as he exchanged proud glances with his wife. The house staff followed in the celebration. Malcolm caught the smiles and looks on their faces. He flashed his "I'm a good boy" smile, letting his bath towel drop to rush by my side. I placed my arm around his waist and brought him close. "I love you. You will always be my baby."

It took Papa several minutes to get a line to the States, and even then I was concerned with the time difference Gbenga may be sleeping and not pick up the phone. He must have answered because Papa moved straight into his conversation with minimal pleasantries. I enjoyed hearing my father in-law speak. The joy bounced around in his mouth landing on the soft spot under my jaw. He smiled at me and handed Momma the phone. I couldn't understand what she said, but as she looked over at me, a tear rolled slowly down her rounded cheek.

"Is it true?" Gbenga asked his voice groggy with sleep.

"I think so," I spoke softly, testing the waters. "I am two weeks late. But I haven't taken a test."

"This is incredible news. The loss of one brings the life of another. It's a sign we are meant to be a family."

"Were you waiting for a sign?"

"I was praying that you would want this marriage as much as I do."

"I didn't give up on us."

When I didn't hear any response right away, I thought the connection was lost. "Gbenga?"

"Yes, I'm here." His tone changed to resignation, which got me thinking. *Maybe he was expecting more enthusiasm on my part. Maybe another baby on the way will sidetrack his promise to stop hustling? That would just be an excuse, if anything he'd understand he has even more to lose.*

"What's on your mind?"

"My mother," he sounded puzzled.

"I think she may still be mourning," I interrupted.

"She has never talked to me that way," he said emphatically. "She told me she will never accept any other woman in our family other than you. She asked me if I had put my hands on you."

"And you said?"

The phone was silent again. "Gbenga?"

"I'm still here." The quiet hesitation in his voice had me rattled. *Maybe he had a taste of the shame I had been holding through the years. Maybe he wanted to change. I am sure he wasn't expecting the verbal lashing his mom gave him, not to her fa-vo-rite child.*

I closed my eyes to shield myself from path of this melancholy cold front sweeping through the line.

"I'm still sleepy," Gbenga said with a deep sigh. "You three come home safely. Bye."

When he hung up, I stood holding onto the receiver until a series of bell tones snapped me loose. I hung up the phone, and tried not to reflect on how his mother's words made him feel. I wanted just a moment to study how it made me feel. I smiled.

A few days later I said goodbye and smiled, considering all Momma had said. I closed my eyes, slowly blinking, capturing her sweet strong image inside my heart. I knew I had responsibilities in this marriage. For better or worse, those were the vows we took. It was upfront, no small print. We weren't in the church, but with God in my heart I repeated those vows. You get through the hard stuff and your reward is around the corner. Something I did or said could bring the worse out in Gbenga. I needed to find out what would push him; because that wasn't the direction I wanted us to go.

Through my entire pregnancy, Gbenga was the ideal husband. We redecorated Malcolm's bedroom and designed a nursery with new furniture and fresh wall color. He attended some of Malcolm's soccer games and cheered more loudly than anyone else on the field. He would go grocery shopping at Whole Foods, never failing to ask me each day if I had taken my vitamins. At night, after he carried Malcolm to sleep, we would curl up with each other on the couch watching television, Gbenga's hands resting against my tummy, as if he wanted to help me carry our baby.

My body showed the evidence, but Gbenga had the nesting symptoms. I was happy his conversations with family in Nigeria became more frequent. He completed the water project for his village and wanted to start developing our "vacation" house. I loved looking through pages of Architectural Digest and Dwell during the design process. He hired his friend Chuks, a Professor and architectural engineer at Prairie View University to render the design. Chuks was able to incorporate our lifestyle passions into a sprawling innovative mansion. Gbenga referred to it as Songhai Estate. Building the house, and all of the excitement it brought to the village, was surely an invitation to his former self, Gbenga Ndili—Ayabingi (I-ya-bing-ee), his friends called him—had been lost to the hustle.

13 Static Electricity

Large night clubs catering to the hip-hop and r& b crowd change so frequently in Columbus and I never cared much for the night scene, if Columbus really has one. Hustlers who have money go out of town to get their party on and girls who "makin' it happen" have few designer boutiques to shop in, so they rock jeans and fur coats, nail tips, and bootleg handbags. I had no desire to be around the "beautiful" people, but I needed music to wash over my mood, bass to hit the lows in my soul and make them groove taking my heart and head along for the ride. I got dressed and decided to hit the Reggae spot on High Street. It was smaller and I'd be less likely to run into someone that would want to make small talk. I hit the doors and the smoke hit me. The vibes seized me, and the music surged through my body. I walked over and rested against the bar. I turned to the bartender and ordered an amaretto sour. I stirred the drink with my cherry and raised it to my lips. I lifted my eyes feeling I was being stared at. I turned my head and saw Scott at the end of the bar. I hadn't seen him for a long time, but he still looked good: a crème café complexion with a basketball player's physique, an edged up five o'clock shadow and deep wavy black hair. He had a cute girl beside him talking in his ear, but he kept looking at me. I smiled and walked closer to where the band was playing. Several of the members from different reggae bands had now formed into a new band. Dashawn, now with sun tipped dreads much longer, was in front belting out roots music with his sweet voice, but the sound was all still the same. They were just wrapping up their second set when I felt some one behind me whisper in my ear, "I had to come over here to see if it was really you." The voice was soft but it harkened a feeling inside of me that started in my chest and got warmer as I took in air into my body. I stared straight ahead with no expression to anyone that was looking at me. "Yea, it's me. Now please go over there and don't make your girlfriend unhappy."

"You know I cannot see you and not speak. Are you staying?" He moved his body in front of mine.

"No, actually I will be leaving soon. I just came to hear some music. It's good seeing you." I put my drink up to my lips and took in the sweetness, the cool burn resurrecting me from the dream-like gaze I felt coming over my face.

"I know you don't think I can let you just walk out of my life again not knowing if it will be years until I see you again? Let me take her home and come back so we can talk."

Both flattered and frustrated I responded, "No, give me your number and I can give you a call tomorrow. I've been on the receiving end of a player and I'm not contributing to anybody's heartache." I turned to look him straight in his eyes. Oooh, I shouldn't have done that.

"Nobody's but mine? 4716329, but there is no way I am taking a chance to see if you are going to call." He walked away and went over to his girlfriend and then over to Dave, a partner of his he used to come into the restaurant with. He handed Dave his keys and with swiftness the girl walked over, waving her finger, saying something in Scott's face and she walked out of the club. The whole scene moved like a stage play. I stopped watching and made a move to the bar to leave, skipping the usual ritual of eating the cherry off its stem.

I walked towards the door when Dashawn softly tugged me by the arm.

"N'wa go on, girl? It's good to see you, how have you been? How's the pi'kin dem, how is my African brethren?" He wrapped his arm around me and pulled me towards him.

"All is good, and you? You sang a nice set." I smiled and moved past him. I could hear him sigh (must have been the way I switched), but I didn't turn around. He always has been an 'ass man.'

Stepping down to the sidewalk the hustle and glare of High Street enticed me to stroll down where my restaurant was once located. Lord knows I needed the air. I don't know if it was the weed, the attention, or the inflexible ripped form of Scott's chest positioned behind me that had me light-headed. I strolled, peering inside store windows, observing changes and redevelopments from drab, dated buildings to quaint art galleries and urban upscale living. The sound of footsteps shifted behind me. I didn't need to look behind me. The smell of the essential oil intertwined with his aroma couldn't camouflage who it was.

He put his hand on my head and ran his fingers through my hair. "You don't deserve this. I know nothing has changed because I see the pain deep in your eyes, but I also still see some of you in there." I could feel each strand of my hair lifting from my scalp and gliding through his fingers. The charge of such a sensual touch was snapping me into a fever. I was struggling to stay in my skin. I was drawn to his eyes, not the color, but the way he held me with them.

"Why wouldn't you let me take you away from that trash?" His hand tenderly brushed between my shoulder blades.

"It wasn't the right time, for you or for me," I said, turning my back to walk the other direction.

"All you had to do is tell me the word. All I have ever wanted was a chance to get closer to you."

"Closer to me or closer to the panties?" I casually looked over my shoulder.

"Girl, I know you are joking. You feel the way I look at you. I still know your birthday, your son's birthday. Can you remember anything about me?" His voice rose as he reached for my hand.

"Scott, you and I have been friends for a long time. You have always been considerate of me, you've never been pushy, but when we met, I was someone's girlfriend and you were someone's man with a baby you thought was your own. Outside of that, I didn't see a need to push it any further." I released his hand and continued to walk towards my car.

"Well, first tell me what's going on? When did you get back?"

We came to my car and stopped walking.

"Two months ago, give or take," I said, as I leaned up against the car.

"Damn, and I am just now seeing you? You didn't know my number? I would have thought we were better than that. We have always been able to talk. I have always cared about you and how you are doin' even if I couldn't have you for myself. Man that cuts, Kim." He looked into my eyes and then looked down at my neck, his eyes scanning my skin. I knew what he saw, but I ignored the question I knew was on the tip of his tongue, and turned to put my key in the door.

"What's going on Kim?"

I didn't turn around. "I'm going home. You know it's not my style to close down the clubs."

He clutched my shoulder slightly. My eyes lifted and I glimpsed at my face reflecting in the car window.

"Kim, what's going on with you? You aren't just visiting, are you?"

"I'm not sure what I am doing, but right now I am going home." He put his arms around my waist and rested against my back as he pulled me into his chest.

"You know I will help you, even if all you will let me do is hold you right here until the sun comes up." I stood there holding back the tears by filling my lungs with the cool night air.

"I left Nigeria. I wanted to come back, but my babies are still there." Seeing the mirror image of myself tore me up inside. There was no more light in my eyes. I was dressed well but the label of parent gave me far more significance than the label of Prada. Anything I heard, smelled, touched, or saw all carried me back to my boys. The vision I wanted to see was not me, but them looking back at me.

"It's been so long since I have seen you. You only had Malcolm. What is your other child's name?"

"Steven." No sooner than my tongue tapped the roof of my mouth than a tear came down. Scott touched my cheek and lifted the tear with the bend of his finger.

"What can we do to get them back?"

"Nothing. He won't give them to me and he certainly wouldn't let them come and visit now that he knows I was trying to take them out or the country."

"Aren't the boys U.S. citizens? Can't the embassy in Nigeria help you get them back?"

My eyes looked over at him as I laughed to myself. "They can't help me get them back. They wouldn't step in when I needed to leave. It's a very complicated system, where oil is the only thing making the headlines. It would take international media attention. How many cameras care to show what is going on in Africa?" Thinking about it made me heated. The anger drew me into the car, guilt creeping on my shoulders. Why am I out, away from my boys? "I'm sorry. It was so good to see you. I need to go home."

Days passed as quickly as the seed heads of the dandelions blew in the summer air. My inside feelings were outside layers of resentment and torment, hardly a good posture to have while looking for work. I could not shed my anguish, and every fleeting smile was followed by an emptiness that couldn't be filled. Crying was no longer sufficient. It had been three weeks since Scott and I saw each other on High Street. We talked nearly every night for hours and he offered to let me use one of his cars so I could fill out applications and drop off resumes. He called during the days to see if I had eaten or to ask me if he could pick me up to grab something to eat. His appeals to help were thoughtful. I knew enough to know that concern showed caring, but I wanted all emotions reserved, saved for my children.

"I'm coming over to get you," Scott's voice was jumping through the phone.

"No, you can't, I'm not ready to go anywhere."

"Put some clothes on and tell me where to pick you up. I'm taking you out," he said, not noticing my opposition.

"It is not about getting dressed. I am dressed! I am just not ready to go out yet."

"Then give me directions and I'll bring you over some curry chicken. It's not yours, but it's pretty good."

"All right, just give me thirty minutes." I hung up the phone, fumbling through suitcases and hefty bags of clothes. "It's not a date," I thought to myself, but I damn sure was ready to shed the pity party apparel for some diva duds. I pulled my luggage from under the bed. I hadn't opened it for weeks because some of the boys' clothes were still inside. I tugged at the contents, looking for anything that would just feel good against my skin. I couldn't work towards looking good, because clothes weren't going to help me pull that off with the way I was feeling. I was going for different, not run of the mill. I skimmed the luggage and noticed a bright covered fabric barely peaking out beneath some jeans.

"Zizi Cardow designs." I shrugged. Baby Phat meets the Motherland, kind of like the fashion child of Kimora and Djimon. I was hoping if I looked good I would feel good. Pulling the skirt over my curves I felt a slight buckle in my knees. I laced the back of the halter, pulling the satin straps snuggly over my shoulders and leaving a bow resting against the small of my back.

The doorbell rang downstairs but I wanted to take one more glance in the mirror. I stood frozen gazing at the figure in front of me. The reflection darted, bending at odd angles, like a funhouse mirror. I reached out but all I felt was space and air. I walked closer to the opening, feeling void, yet familiar. I leaned in, peering at the image. What I saw was not what I expected. What I saw was me.

"Sooky sooky mama, you're looking good, Kimmy," my cousin Stacy laughed. "Still need to put on a little more weight, but that ass is back."

"Girl stop," I said nudging her hip with my hip. "I just want to lay this stuff down for a minute, long enough to catch my breath." No sooner had the words come out of my mouth, I remembered what Gbenga said, hovering over me as a lay like a wad of cookie dough on the floor… "appreciate your breath, while you still got some left." With that, I turned to go downstairs.

"You need to lay it down, but don't give up the good good while ya laying," she snickered.

"Girl, I got enough, I don't need to add to my problems." I thought about making him wait for a minute, but why bother, this was not a date. I reached the top of the stairs and saw Scott standing there with a huge bouquet of white and purple cala lilies. He looked casually fine in faded jeans, slight sag, blue button down shirt, with a white tee barely peeking above the top button. I spoke inside my head: "Damn, this is not supposed to be a date. This sure feels like it's a date." He must have read it all over my face.

"Before you say it, I know this is not a date." Scott handed me the flowers. I just thought you could have them around to look at, to remind you to not to scowl all the time."

"I don't scowl."

"Hmph, yes, you have been," Stacy interjected, "ever since you got here."

"Thanks!" I held the flowers to my nose inhaling the sweet balsamic fragrance.

"You're welcome," they both said at the same time.

"I appreciate the flowers, Scott. Just so we're clear, it's two friends going out kickin' it."

"Yep, two friends. I just think you need to get out of the house and give your mind a rest. No one is trying to get in your pants," he said holding the door open, swinging in the brisk air. "Then again, you aren't wearing pants," his mouth twisted in a half smile.

"Indeed, I'm not, and if you would like to keep what is swinging inside yours, you'll understand that is not where I am right now," rolling my eyes and neck with the same attitude as my voice.

"Understood. Now that's the feisty Kim I knew was still in there."

We rode for a while, when I noticed we were pulling off Morse Road into a housing subdivision. "Where are we going?"

"We're going to get something to eat," turning down the jazz on the radio. "Is that cool?"

"Yeah," I said, a little perplexed at the location. "But uh, these are houses."

As we pulled into a driveway, "And this is my house," he announced, then got out and walked around the car to get my door.

"Your house?"

"Tonight, someone is going to take care of you for a change," he interjected, gently holding my hand as he walked me up the stairs, pausing at the landing. "Go up the steps to your right. Take as long as you need. I need to finish dinner."

"Upstairs?" I felt uncomfortable as he guided my hand onto the banister. Slowly, I continued up the steps, following a trail of tiny votive candles, each flicker ushering me down the hallway. My hand clenched as I pressed the door open. Shadows flickered in crimson light against the wall. A king-size bed headlined the room, dressed with Egyptian linen and slightly elevated on an oak-stained platform. My hands started to turn cold from nerves when I noticed a large pink Victoria's Secret bag lying on the bed. "What the hell?" crossed my mind as I stepped closer to the bed. I glanced inside and saw a white terry robe poking beneath the tissue paper. Was this a preparation to some kind of foreplay?

"Scott!"

His cologne announced his entrance, "I already know what you are thinking and the answer is no."

"No, what?"

"No, I am not taking you home. No, I did not bring you here to get ass, and no, this is not a set- up move."

"You have no idea what I am thinking, because it cannot be

answered with a simple no. What am I supposed to do with this?" I questioned, pulling the robe out of the bag and tossing it over to him.

"I wanted to bring you here so you can relax," as he unfolded the robe, "and someone can take care of you for a minute."

"This is thoughtful, but I'm more comfortable relaxing with my clothes on. I don't want to confuse issues."

"What is confusing about getting in some you time? I don't want anything from you and this is long overdue. I have an opportunity to show you how you should be treated. Maybe it's just been so long, you forgot what it feels like." He pushed the robe into my hands. "I'll lock the door. Come out when you're ready."

I nodded reluctantly.

We didn't say another word to each other. My heart stopped for a brief second, still remembering I had one. I followed the sounds of music coming from the back of the room into the adjoining bathroom. I sat on the edge of the bathtub gazing at the iridescent foam. I wanted to get in and be covered from my toes to my head, but I didn't want to be naked, to the water or to him. I love taking a bath, being totally wrapped up in it, with the ease of freedom in motion. I tried to turn the door knob, testing to see if it was locked. Taking off my clothes, I crawled in, allowing the comforting warm water to envelope and caress me. My eyes were closed and my mind was free. I added more hot water, hoping to soak through to my bones. I lay still, hearing the tiny crackling of bubbles as they exposed themselves to the air. Time passed, until one island of suds was left in the sea full of water.

I stood up, tying the robe around my waist. Walking downstairs I noticed his house was full of original paintings and numbered prints, not the typical framed posters sold at the annual street festivals and black book stores. Scott was standing in the kitchen, the over head light from the stove top outlined his chiseled body. "I didn't know you cook?"

"I don't really, but I can read. I picked up some fish and grabbed one of those recipe cards from the counter. I know I can't beat the queen of the kitchen, he poked as he pulled the foil back from the steamy dish, but you won't leave hungry."

"It smells good. I see you are full of surprises this evening."

"I don't know why you are surprised; all I ever needed was an opportunity."

"The artwork, the style of the kitchen, did you do all of it?"

"I remember some of the art you had at the restaurant you told me you bought or ordered from Black Arts Plus on Parsons. I bought most of it there, some at the Columbus Art festival and asked the owner to come to the house and hang it. Do you like it?"

"Yeah, I do and I am surprised you even remembered" I blushed with a slight smile.

We finished our dinner and went on talking for hours about the time he saw me buying supplies for the restaurant at Sam's Club, Ice Breakers at the Ohio Union, clubbin' at Papa Jacks and Headliners, the time he bought

Malcolm a truck for his first birthday, and the first time he ate Red Snapper at my restaurant. Laughs came out from places so deep inside of me. It felt like the blood running through my body was carbonated and opening my mouth sent bubbles tickling my nose and gums. I pushed off on his shoulder during the last hysterical fit and he countered resting his hand on my forearm.

"What makes you happy?"

"What?"

"What do you like to do?"

"I don't know" I was covering my crossed legs with the robe and stopped. "I am not really sure what I like to do anymore." Playing it back in my head, my eyes filled up. I wasn't sure what I was feeling. I was just glad I was feeling.

He looked deep into my eyes. We didn't move or say another word to each other. Our kiss began, getting deeper and softer at the same time and to this day, I have no idea where it came from. My eyes were closed, but I kept staring into the eyes of the reflection standing across from me upstairs. I'm starting to like what I see, or is it what I feel? I was floating.

I was trying to get out of there before my mind was swept away by flustered emotions. Scott broke the silence, speaking softly leaning towards my neck, "I'm here" his warm breath ticking my ear with every syllable. His lips grabbed for my earlobe, diamond studs included, as his tongue grazed just seconds before I pulled away.

"I need to go home," my voice scratched as the words left my mouth. "Now please."

"Alright, I will get your clothes."

I scurried to the bathroom mumbling a fury of prayers while getting dressed. It's hard to have selfish thoughts while prayin', keep praisin', keep prayin'.

I came out of the bathroom as he stood by the front door with his coat on, hand running back and forth over the soft curls in his fade as if to iron his thoughts away.

"I can't start something new with more questions than answers." I sighed.

"But I am here Kim, to help you put the pieces together," he replied, as he took my hand and gently kissed the tips of my fingers.

Something snapped inside of me causing me to drop my hand. "I don't want to start with pieces. I want to be whole." There was a piece wanting to learn what went wrong in my marriage and the boys had a piece of me back there with them, and they were pieces I felt I couldn't live without it.

We barely said anything on the ride home. "Thanks for everything tonight Scott, sorry it didn't turn out maybe as you expected."

"You're welcome, and it did. I only wanted you to smile and think about what you deserve. Call me if you want to talk." He returned to his car as I stood back turned fidgeting with the lock and key until the headlights slowly dimmed down the driveway.

I thought about calling him every day after that night, teetering with feelings of butterflies and the guilt of laughter in the absence of my boys. I would sit some days up in the bed with the blanket pulled over my shoulders. I sighed and imagined his shoulders and body touching against my side. I closed my eyes and tried to imagine his laughter, his smile and the interest he had in what made me happy. I would pull the covers so tightly I could feel the stitching in the blanket across my knuckles. I shook my shoulders. Eventually I stopped seeing the mistakes in the reflection between me and the mirror and held on to the love I knew I was capable of having.

Gbenga wired $3,000 to repay the Embassy and replace my visa. He also sent a round trip ticket in my name, hoping to put the family at ease about my return. I bought a new Nintendo game system and new clothes for the boys along with two Thomas Pink dress shirts for Gbenga. I thought about a few more things I could pick up, but I kept fifty dollars in my wallet for the flight back and tucked two hundred dollar bills behind my driver's license in my wallet.

I laid my luggage on the bed. A daunting feeling came over me the very moment I placed my clothes inside. I have a routine when packing; heaviest things on the bottom, followed by the lighter ones to prevent wrinkling. Layer after layer, similar to my relationship, heavy hurt layered with peripheral fluff.

As the last pair of panties was laid on the top of the bag, I zipped the bag closed and kneeled down to pray. *Thank you Lord for the opportunity to hold my babies again. Lord, you know more than I what I am facing. I pray that your will be done. Help me to go back to Gbenga with a clear mind. Change me so I can see what needs to be done. Grant me ears so I can hear your direction. Amen.*

I picked my bag up, took a deep breath. *God, you got this.*

Sticky Notes

I arrived at the ticket counter smiling as I placed my passport on top of my ticket and handed them to the ticket agent.

"You don't have a visa."

"Yes, ma'am, I do. I have a resident visa, if you look at the attached passport." I turned the pages until I reached the back of the passport.

I remembered all that the Wives went through regarding alien status; marching, petitioning, protesting. Every branch of Wives fought in some way. I regarded that time as my own freedom march, so that little piece of paper held a great deal of significance.

I stopped to pick up a couple magazines on my way to the gate: InStyle for fashion; (the tailors in Nigeria can duplicate any style with a picture) and O magazine, for the substance. Television programming was limited; Jerry Springer, Cheaters, Sex in the City and Oprah the only American entertainment you can find worth watching in Africa. I handed my boarding pass to the man at the gate. He smiled and uttered something, "Have a nice flight" or something like that, but I could not take my eyes off of the ramp leading to the plane. People seem to go around the corner and disappear. You can see the ramp looking out the window leading to the plane, but as you approach to board, you don't see the entrance into the plane. You only see the ramp and hear the hollow sound of luggage being dragged behind you. I felt like I was about to be swallowed. My legs slowed down and my heart sped up. Then I saw the friendly smile of a steward standing inside the plane. "Good afternoon, can I check your ticket?" I snapped back to reality and took my seat.

The flight was nice. For eight hours I thought about the words Gbenga said and imagined our Sundays jet-skiing, high seas fishing and playing on the beach with the kids. I wrote down ideas about starting my own business and the ways I could market it. I thought about the first thing I wanted to eat when I got to Lagos. I smiled and pushed deeper into my seat.

The taxi drove into Victoria Island, pulled around the corner of Duro Sinmi Etti, and slowed down. I could see the boys playing basketball outside. I reached down to get my purse, and as I turned my head around I saw the most mesmerizing pair of mahogany brown eyes looking into mine through the taxi window.

"It's Mommy!" Steven shouted as he jumped and pointed around the taxi. Like an eager child tailing behind an ice cream truck.

My heart was full and my smile took over my face from ear to ear. I opened the door and lifted my baby high in the air, bringing him down with a big kiss. Ibrahim came outside from the security house and greeted me as he took my bags into the house. The nanny ran outside through the gate and nearly bowled me over with a hug.

"Oh Madam, it is good to see you, welcome, welcome!" Her voice was full and came out squeezed between her teeth.

As I was sandwiched between Steven and the nanny, my eyes looked up and overflowed with tears. Standing ten feet away, holding a basketball under his arm, long legs and a face like mine was Malcolm. The beating of my heart hadn't quite caught up with my breath when I moved to walk towards him. I wasn't sure what to make of his slow pace walking towards me. Was he in shock? Did my absence make him resent me? He seemed to have gotten so grown in a little over six months. I opened my arms to give him a hug and he stopped less than six inches from me. He looked up at me and saw the tears running down my face. He bent down and reached for his sock. He came up and opened his hand. "Well, I guess you'll want this back." It was the rattiest looking dollar bill I had ever seen. I smiled and we hugged each other tightly, my tears falling on the top of his round head.

Ibrahim handed the taxi driver some money and immediately I knew Gbenga was aware I was back. I looked up to the balcony and he smiled as he caught a glimpse of my face. I smiled with my lips together, each one of my arms wrapped around the boys. I grabbed my purse and we strolled up towards the house as Steven told me about everything I missed the last three months in under two and a half minutes, without taking a breath.

Gbenga opened the door and unlocked the gate, for a moment I looked at his smile and wanted to fall deep into his arms, but I couldn't. I wasn't ready to let go of the boys just yet, or let my guard down yet either. The lawn hadn't been watered. It was balding, grass grown tough and wispy, and it had given way in several patches to brown sandy earth. I walked in the door, same marble floors glistening, same silk flowers in the entry way, same oil paintings on the walls. This house was too lovely not to be a home, I remember each and every collectible that sat on the shelf, and the significance they held. They were now covered with dust, a small indication of my absence. All of it had appeared more vivid in my memories, when I left them behind.

The smell of onions frying in palm oil filled the dining room. The aroma of egusi soup was being carried on the wind as it crept through the kitchen window. Other than some small details, that I am sure only I noticed, the house seemed to have kept running. One of the advantages of having a house staff. But I sensed it trifled my absence. I walked up the stairs, Malcolm still holding my hand. I expelled the hours of anticipation that had built up to this moment as I sat on the couch staring at my luggage. Malcolm and Steven leaned up against the wall with fleeting glances, awaiting the treasures that could be inside my suitcase. I noticed them and stood up, stretching my back side to side.

"Mommy, Malcolm said you brought us something from the U.S.? Did you, Mommy?"

"Oooh, I am still so tired baby, let's wait until tomorrow." I turned to walk upstairs.

"We can get it, Mom," Steven said as he sprang to the bag.

"That's all right Steven. I'll get it after I have had a bath." His face was shattered and he sank deep into the couch. I laughed and turned around, kneeling to open the trunk, which carried some games for them, and some I reserved for Malcolm's birthday. Nothing spoils a reunion faster than a video game.

There I was no diversions, just me and Gbenga. He was my husband but I was hoping to see my friend. I walked over to where he was sitting on the couch. He put his arm around me. I tried to fall back; back into those broad shoulders, folded into his chest. But I was flat, indifferent about the promises he made, tired from traveling more than twenty hours and at least seventeen of them were spent mapping out the bruises, the scars, and the partial hearing loss in my left ear. I put my hand on his knee, caressing the bend with my fingers, reminiscing about a happier time when I was his biggest cheerleader and his water girl while he played soccer on the fields in Houston. My thoughts were broken by the rhythmic sounds of yam being pounded downstairs in the kitchen. I looked at Gbenga with a grin and stood. "I'm going to take a bath and change."

I walked upstairs to the master bedroom. The dark cherry sleigh bed had been made and turned down on one side as they do in some hotels. The sun had set and the quiet ocean breeze danced with the palm fronds outside the balcony. I gazed at the bougainvillea in beautiful bloom as it camouflaged the compound wall; covered by the darkness they had an elegant poetry. Familiar sounds of okadas stopping on the street to drop off market women who were finishing their work for the day echoed close-by. I closed the balcony door and the stale air filled the room. I pressed the menu button on the air conditioner remote, but it did not respond. I continued to the bathroom and adjusted the water for my bath. I sat on the edge of the tub, let my head back and sighed with contentment. The giggles in the background were like balm soothing my heartache. But my heart was not yet filled. Questions came like drops of water and before I knew it I had a reservoir of reservations. Immersed in water, I sank until the wet danced around my ears and drowned out the voices in my head. Muffled, soaked in a state of fluidity, a condition I long for when I am stressed, but it echoes my yearning for Gbenga. Just seeing his face, I realize that when I am near him I can never just take a dip and stick my toe in to test the water. It's a plunge, he permeates me from outside in, oblivious to all that I am absorbing.

A tap at the door broke my meditation. "Madam, food is ready."

I came out of the water with a towel wrapped around me. Warm winds from the balcony swept around my body and through my hair. I dropped my towel to put on lotion. I leaned over, applying shea butter to my legs when sudden movement caught my attention. Gbenga came in from the balcony, resting against the frame in the door.

"You know, I thought maybe we could go away for a few days, just me and you."

I reached on the bed to grab my towel. "Oh yeah, well, I haven't been around the boys for a while, so I just want to enjoy them." Feeling like a woman naked for the first time in front of a man she was arranged to marry, I coyly wrapped the thick terry cloth towel around my body, tucking it beneath my arm.

"Looks like you added a little weight?" His eyes scanning over my backside.

"Yea, maybe a little."

"It looks good. I like it. I need for you to put on some weight. I want you to be happy."

"This sure didn't come from being happy. It came from fried chicken and biscuits at Popeyes. I was never in the mood to cook. It only made me think of the boys." I bent down to look in my luggage for a pair of panties.

"Those are nice, are they new?" The question was above suspicion, but reflection triggered feelings of hesitation. "Yeah, I went to get a few things before coming back."

"Yeah, it was the hardest thing going into the guest room seeing your thongs hanging on the clothesline without thinking of the way those curves looked when I would see you with them on." He placed his hand on his khaki shorts, holding firm to the bulge beneath the crease. My hands grew clammy.

"So where did you want to go? Maybe we can take the boys out somewhere?" I talked while getting dressed.

"Just me and you, I want us to talk. I just want to be with you, baby. I can get Nkem or Ufoma to watch the boys. I am sure they will understand that their father and mother need to be alone. We haven't seen each other in some time." He walked towards me, eyes looking into my face.

My body was tense. I wasn't ready for us to be alone. "Gbenga, baby, I am back now, but you and I have a lot to work on. I want us to move slowly; get to know each other again. Remember all of the things that made us fall in love in the beginning."

"We can do that, but I really want to show you Abuja. It is beautiful. If I knew it was this beautiful we would have moved there, and not to Lagos."

My mind drifted. I love the beauty that is in different lands. I enjoy seeing the change in the land formations and the woodlands. The vibrancy and distinction of different cultures, from the dressing to the hair adornments, to the markings etched in their faces. It's like seeing a well-stitched quilt, sewing us all together, living and breathing in God's marvels.

"Alright, time alone may be what we need. I'll go." Reservation was replaced with a need to refill my soul, but for now, my stomach would have to do.

Gbenga smiled as we went downstairs, I missed that smile, that tiny gap in between his straight front teeth, mouth parted just enough to see his tongue. The aroma of egusi soup and pounded yam tickled my nose as I came to the landing by the living room. I sat in front of the tray. No sooner had grace had left my tongue than I pulled a piece of fufu to knead between my fingers. I dipped it in the hearty soup and let it fall to my stomach. Steven came to sit by my side. I took him on my lap, smiling and licking our fingers until we could see the bottom of the bowl. I pushed the tray to the center of the table. I washed my hands in the bowl of water. Steven splashed his fingers and ran on to his room. Gbenga called Ibrahim from the balcony. The last ray of sun was tucked away by the blanket of night. The cool winds had already begun lifting the waves on the Atlantic. I stood on the balcony, a melody of dreamy sounds rumbling from Bar Beach. The horns flowed from a familiar afro-beat track, while "white garment followers" merged drums and chanting while performing water rituals. Gbenga stood beside me. I reached for his hand.

"Baby, it's our time. Me and you together could do so much here," he said and looked into my eyes tenderly. "Remember what we built out of Columbus? In a short time, we sewed it up."

Not quite the soliloquy I had hoped for at that moment, but I knew what he was trying to say. "Gbenga, baby, I never had any doubt that you will make it in business, all of that lifestyle before. Your dreams were much bigger and you are much smarter than what you were getting into. I only wanted us. When we did have all of that money, the cars, we never enjoyed it. You will make it in Nigeria. It is just going to take some faith and time."

The balcony door opened, Esther was carrying a plastic serving tray with plates and a package covered in newspaper. That package was the one thing that could lure the boys away from their video games. SUYA! Malcolm and Steven came to sit at the table on the balcony just waiting for me to open the bundle. I let it sit there for a moment, amused by their restlessness. Gbenga was the first to break and went over to open it up. Succulent skewers of roasted meats seasoned with ground peanuts and spices, wrapped up with slices of red onion and ground pepper. The bite from the stout inflamed the spices in Gbenga's mouth and he liked it. You really value the flavor when the walls of your mouth tingle and your nose starts to run.

After a bellyfull we sat down on the leather sofas to watch Channel O. It's similar to MTV, but in color; assortments of music videos from Africa, Latin America, the Caribbean, and various African-American artists. Jet lag caught up with me, as I dozed off feeling the sweat from my body heat like adhesive to the leather. I stood, picking up Steven, his chubby legs dangling as I balanced his butt on one arm. The change in positions stirred Malcolm and he reached out for my hand.

"Mom, can you sleep in our room?" I held his thin fingers, as we walked into the room. Steven was still sound asleep, as I laid him down on his bed and covered him with his Scooby Doo comforter. I tucked Malcolm in his bed and lay down beside him.

"So big boy, what did you want to do for your birthday?" I smiled as I brushed against his face with the palm of my hand.

"I want you to make me a layer cake, I want to have a party, and mom," he turned in his sheets to face me. "Mom, I'm glad you are back." His arm fell across me, and I was motionless, except for the tears chasing the pillow from the corners of my eyes.

I was snatched from my sleep by the pulsation coming from the generator. I was now officially back in Lagos- power outages and lines at the gas stations, ceremonial compliments from a government trying to get its legs back. My feet touched the cool marble floor; electricity must not have been off long. I slid from Malcolm's bed on to my knees. "Lord, thank you. Precious Father, thank you for allowing me to see these sweet faces once again. Change me, allow your will to be done, reveal truth. Amen." I stood up gazing at the boys, holding them thoughtfully with my eyes.

Gbenga was sleeping on the couch. He was wearing his khakis and a white t, still holding a cigarette in his hand. I watched as the smoke rose sluggishly upward then scattered invisibly beneath the blades of the ceiling fan. As the waft of smoke passed over, the ash glowed with slivers of heat. Seeing the shine made the hairs on the back of my neck recall being singed and then the smoldering numbness that followed. I took the cigarette between my two fingers and put it out in the ashtray. Gbenga woke up and took a hold of my calf. Time stood still as my breath warmly rushed over my lips and I felt my heart beating beneath my cotton t-shirt. He let up his grip and ran his fingers slowly down my Achilles tendon. I sensed coordination back into my leg and I lifted up my heel to pass in front of him.

"Are the boys asleep?" He asked, propping his back up on the couch.

"Yes, both of them are fast asleep." I passed to sit down on the chair.

"You know I don't know how you do it?"

I looked. "Do what?"

"How you get them ready on time, fix their food." His voice trailed and I leaned forward resting my elbows on my knees clasping my hands.

"I just do. You can too, but when I am doing it, you choose not to." My eyebrows raised and a smile came to my face.

"Well, I got them to school every day and we never ran late, but I had no idea whose uniform was whose, what they liked to eat, or what they wear to bed. Every day I was exhausted." He sat up reaching for the

Benson and Hedges cigarettes on the coffee table.

"Gbenga, ten years and you changed a diaper once, once! You don't bathe them and surely have no idea what they are allergic to, how many shots they have had, or which type of ice cream they like from Chocolate Royale?"

"I know, but all of that is going to change. I missed you so much. I really want my family back." He got up to go to open the door to the balcony. "I even made a decision to smoke outside, because I know my smoking gets to you."

Small changes, but at that time I was just concerned with the mosquitoes he was about to let in. Malaria is nothing nice.

"Gbenga, I know you are a good father, I know your intention is to have the best for your children. But all they ever wanted was you. If my leaving did something for the bond between the three of you, then I am happy. Did you think I wanted to take them with me just to spite you? We talked about this several times. I had to go like that. You told me you would kill me. I never told you I was the better parent, but I know our boys. I didn't think leaving them here to be raised by a nanny while you go out and conquer the world was the best thing."

"Yes, you have raised them, and it scared me that I didn't know how much I don't know about them, but they are my boys." Smoke left from his nostrils as he took the last drag of his cigarette and threw it onto the balcony and closed the door.

"Gbeng, remember when I asked you to pick one day a week for just you and the boys so I could have a day to rejuvenate?"

"Umm-hmm."

"Well, that didn't work, so then I asked for one day out of the month, just for you to write it on the calendar, 'BOYS DAY', one day a month. Well that came and went. I would end up making excuses about you being busy at work, but you would come flying around the corner, top off the jeep, t-shirt off, reggi raae blasting, and no brief case to speak of. We just weren't your priority."

"You are my priority. You'll see. I want to show you how much I love you."

I wondered if he ever rationalized that I loved him so much that it was easier for me to endure the pain of him hurting me than to watch him give up on himself. My physical pain could be isolated to a specific area; the pain of hopelessness in his eyes when he wasn't living up to his own expectations of himself, hurt me to my soul. With that I went up and lay on the bed. I stared at the ceiling for some time until the light off the wall sconces blurred my eyes.

15 Velcro

Riding into Abuja was breath taking. The roads were clear and the landscape was such a contrast to the unrest of Lagos. Gbenga pointed out Abuja's zoning of green areas throughout the city. These weren't really parks, just sections of green land with plants, palms, and grass. The first thing I noticed, or didn't notice, was the lack of danfos crowding the streets over seen by colorful conductors screaming out street names at the top of their lungs. Danfos are a form of local transport in Lagos; bright yellow-colored rickety Volkswagon buses, some resembled a hodge podge of metal scrap thrown together with people sitting humpback to butt crack on the tattered vinyl seats, hurrying to get nowhere. The signs that read "Eko o ni baje," Yoruba for "Don't spoil Lagos," were not posted on every corner. The streets in Abuja were smooth, paved with lines and working traffic lights. We got into the city and it came alive. It smelled like money. The NNPC Headquarters with reflecting glass stood high against the skyline. The Naval building was an architectural tour de force; I had never seen a functional design mimic such a vision. This is where Abuja lost its calm. Gbenga was telling me how the city had grown in population from 350,000 to 2.8 million people in less than ten years. We passed a small market where women sat in shapeless skirts on makeshift stools under colorful umbrellas selling everything from fabric and fruit to flip- flops. Nicon Plaza mimicked any strip plaza you might see in the U.S. My eyes took in the crisp panorama as we entered the Three Arm Zone, the government district, rooted at the foot of the mountainous Zuma Rock. It exuded intimidation and strength just by its placement. The occasional overawing caravan of diplomats would pass along the street, black on black tinted Peugeots followed by stately Range Rovers bearing government license plates and flashing red lights. The House of Assembly building was majestic; similar to the White House, pristine white structure but topped with a vivid green dome adorning the Nigerian flag. Gbenga stopped briefly at the House of Representatives to greet some friends he had gone to secondary school with. As they were talking, I couldn't hear what he was saying. His hands and his voice were battling each other, caressing and challenging the words from his friends. I thought about the pleasure of his voice when he spoke, weaving `into the conversation, speaking to each one as if they are the only person in the room. He paused to look at me like a coy boy, wide-eyed with sweet confidence.

"This is the beautiful queen I cannot live without."

I smiled and after casual introductions we left to go back to the hotel. On our way we passed the Abuja National Stadium, which had just been built for the All Africa games. We moved slowly, gazing at this grand arena as misplaced as a U.F.O. landing in the middle of a cow pasture. The dome cost hundreds of millions of dollars in a country that still cannot provide simple infrastructure and drinkable water to its entire people.

We got to the hotel; three stories of crisp egg shell color, detailed wood finishes and open air reception areas. We walked down the breezeway to our room. Gbenga reached back to grab my hand. My feet lifted and my shoulders settled down. It tickled me how an act so casual and common could seem weird and wonderful. It had been a long time since I had received such a sweet gesture. As he opened the door he smiled gently at me, carrying my breath with his eyes. The room was plush, with simple, sharp white linens. I felt comfort in the fact that we had two beds, so I sat on one and pulled off my sandals.

"You want to order room service or would you like to go out and eat?" He closed the door and picked up the room service card from the table.

"Could we go and eat downstairs?" I contemplated having private time, but I wanted to talk, and people provided safety.

"Sure, I want to shower first and then we can go."

I listened to the water in the shower as it ran, imagining it cooling his head and flowing down his broad shoulders. I came off of the bed, stretching my mind and my body to release itself to a new beginning. I pressed my toes into the fibers of the carpet… like a tree planted at the rivers of water…I could remember Psalms 1:3 in my head.

I grinned, hearing Gbenga belt out a Bob Marley tune in the shower. The songs he sang so often revealed his mood. This was a good day.

We went downstairs to the restaurant and were seated right away.

"Baby, they have a really nice buffet, but you can have whatever you want."

African soups and Chinese dishes filled my plate, while Gbenga feasted on spiced fish and rice. Our conversation was light and I noticed he intensely kept looking at my face.

"When did you stop laughing? You don't have a sense of humor anymore," he said as he reached over the table for my hand.

"Our life stopped being funny a long time ago. Now it seems like a bad joke." I used my hand to place my napkin on lap.

I watched closely as his words gyrated out of his mouth. "I want to start over, I want us to trust and fall in love again. I want my lover and my friend."

"I want to give the boys a mother and father who love them, know how to love each other and can teach them how to love themselves." I don't think I wanted a response, or if I would have believed it if he did. But taking everything I have ever said to him in more than ten years, nothing took more out of me.

We got to the hotel room and I gazed over at the beds. I decided to turn down the covers on the bed closest to the bathroom. Sometimes my system needs a few days to adjust to the food and water.

"You know, neither of these beds compares to the one at home," he expressed while sitting on the corner of the bed.

"Hmm, I know. I loved that bed," I said, picking up the thread of the conversation.

"And it loved you."

"It couldn't have loved me. It never even felt what I was feeling."

"But didn't you love the way it held you?"

"I did, once, but where will we be when we wake up?" I wondered, rubbing my hand against the scalloped squares of the quilted comforter.

"We will be in each other's arms."

I sat looking at the plush fibers in the carpet. It was woven and soft, but I wondered, given the terrain, how much dust might lie underneath.

"We will be all right," he continued. "You have always talked to me about forgiveness and letting go so you can receive your blessings...well, let it go. I am not the same. Something changed in me when I realized you really may not come back." He held me with tender attention, letting go when I didn't respond.

"I decided to forgive as soon as I got on the plane to come here, and God knows leaving was harder than coming back." Reluctantly, I wrapped my arms over his, knowing exactly where my fingers would lace through his.

We lay down, not saying another word, just caught in holding on.

Back in Lagos I woke up to get the boys ready for school. They loved to eat fried plantain and porridge in the morning, but this time I wanted to make them pancakes. They ran downstairs, the soles of their shoes slapping against the marble floors. I laughed at Steven who still rushed through buttoning his shirt, making one side longer than the other. They ate and smiled, each laugh like a balm soothing a wound beneath my skin. The two of them had a language to themselves. I was touched to see the closeness that developed between them.

"These are pancakes!" Malcolm chimed, his mouth gaped open with food.

"Mm-hmm, flap jacks, not flip flops like the ones Esther made." Steven chuckled, showing his syrup drizzled tongue to the nanny.

"Now, you all eat up, so Mr. Mathew can drive you to school on time, and Mommy will be there to pick you up." Steven ran to get his sneakers while Malcolm held me tightly at my waist. I leaned, kissing him on the top of his head. "I'm here, and when you get out of school I will be right there. I love you." As if I was reading the questions in his mind.

For some time I had become very good at staying out of Gbenga's way. After all, our house in Lagos was big, and with the staff not used to being in the house until late afternoon when the children arrived, no one would think it strange for me to spend long hours in the guest room reading. I walked, savoring the empty house. I went upstairs to my bedroom. It was a large bright room, 24 feet long by 30 wide with highly polished marble floors. The floor-to-ceiling windows overlooked the front landscape and the tops of a few tin roofs belonging to squatters, which framed my view of the pearly sands and the Atlantic Ocean. This was my sanctuary. I sat frozen in time, the sheers flowing and tagging the sun, as my thoughts drifted. Midway through the morning I felt hungry. I walked to the kitchen to roast some banana. I turned on the oven, opened the door, but the inside broiler wasn't lit.

"Esther! Ibrahim, can you please bring me some matches?" I called towards the back of the house. "Esther, hello?" No one responded. I went to open the back door, but found it locked. I walked to the front of the house, opened the door, but found the security gate locked from the outside. "Ibrahim!" I hollered toward the gatehouse.

"Madam," he responded, thrusting the gatehouse door open.

"Ibrahim, do you have the key to unlock the door?"

"No, madam, the girl locked it when she don come out."

I walked in the house, pacing in circles as I wondered; how long was locking me inside part of the routine? How many days had I spent cleaning the glass on all of the collectibles on the shelves that were neglected in my absence? How many weeks did I spend hunched over a computer researching business models and product development in cellular phone sales to support your business contracts?

I picked up my cell phone to call Gbenga at work. "Hi. Do you think you could come to the house?"

"I am in the middle of writing a proposal to NNPC for a solar panel project. I can send Mathew to bring you to the office."

"I am locked in the house," I took a deep breath. "Was this your way to make sure I didn't go anywhere?"

"What—" he asked, his voice faltering. "I am on my way."

I heard the fast pace of Gbenga's stride as he came around the back door. "Kimmy," he called.

I stared at his face through the window, absorbing the angst in his tone. I was angry, but at the moment it seemed secondary. Abruptly, he flung open the door, rattling off frustrations to Ibrahim in Hausa. He walked in the kitchen and grimaced. Like a knee-jerk reaction I fixed a smile on my face. "Esther must have been in the habit of locking the door when she goes out," I said softly, absolving. "She must have assumed I had a key."

The lines in between Gbenga's eyebrows smoothed. Startlingly—I realized when he was calmer, I was more at ease too.

Gbenga caressed my face with his palms. "Sorry-o, no vex," he said apologetically, as he removed his key from the ring and handed it to me. "I want you here with me. I want you here because you want to be. I am not interested in having under lock and key. I love you."

"I am here because I want to be," I spoke softly, squeezing his fingers. "I was going to fix something to eat before I pick up the boys."

"I will send Mathew to pick them up."

"That's o.k. I haven't seen them at school in months. It will give me the opportunity to catch up with the Headmistress and their teachers. Weren't you in the middle of work?"

"This is more important. Let's go together."

"Great. The boys haven't had the two of us pick them up. They will be surprised."

We pulled outside the large iron-gate at Kemson International School. Drivers were gathered in knots along the campus wall, exchanging quips and gossips about current events. A chubby faced girl with neatly parted cornrows appeared in her uniform. Her white lace knee socks dusty from time spent on the playground. She stretched her arm high to grab the rope attached to the school bell. She pulled back and forth, the beads in her hair competing for attention with the ring of the bell. Immediately the sounds of children's voices could be heard rolling through the classrooms.

Gbenga and I stood outside the classroom waiting for Steven to turn around. He placed his papers in the inbox of his teacher's desk, spun around and caught a glimpse of us.

"Mummy!" he shouted and ran. "Mummy, I didn't know you and Daddy were both coming." His eyes were wide with excitement.

"We wanted to surprise you," Gbenga said, lifting him high in the air.

"Did you do well in school today?" I asked.

"I did well in school today," he responded laughing, his limbs dangling in the air.

I gave a small wave to his teacher and walked out to the car.

Traffic through the roundabout was slow. As we pulled on Mekunwen Road you could see cars lining up to leave Corona. Girls were playing hand games and hop scotch with small rocks. The boys were lined up on the playground, a line in the sand beneath their feet. "Ready, set, go!" They were running full force to the cones in the near distance. Clouds of dust followed them as shouts, "Up Weaver! Up Crane!" echoed on the sidelines. I remembered this time of year. The boys were preparing for the Corona Inter-House Sports Day.

We got out of the car. Steven spotted a man approaching on a bicycle with shaved ice in his basket. As Gbenga approached to buy Steven a shaved ice, I walked into the courtyard to look for Malcolm.

"Can I help you Madam?" A young coffee brown woman approached me, her hair cut low in a natural afro.

"Yes. I am picking up my son Malcolm Ndili." I continued to scan the playing faces on the grounds when I heard a loud whistle. Seconds passed and I saw the Head Mistress, Mrs. Agbade, walking in my direction. "Good afternoon," I greeted.

"Good afternoon," she replied, in a low monotone with a stern look on her face.

"It's good to see you. How have you been?"

"I have been well. Are you coming to get Malcolm?"

"Yes ma'am."

"I'm sorry. I cannot let you do that."

"Excuse me?"

"I cannot let you take Malcolm. We have specific instructions that he is only allowed to leave with the driver."

I couldn't believe what I was hearing. "What?" I looked, tilting my head to one side. "I am his mother, and I am coming to take him home."

"I'm sorry. I cannot let you take him." She said standing in front of me.

I turned to see Gbenga, Steven and the driver walking through the gate. I swung my purse over my shoulder and faced Gbenga with my hand on my hip. At the same time, Malcolm sprinted across the school yard throwing his sweaty arms around me.

"Mom, you came!"

I was still frozen in anger. I was afraid of what would come out of my mouth, so I kissed Malcolm's salty forehead and left Gbenga there to work it out. I took one last look over my shoulder at the Head Mistress smiling at Gbenga and rolled my eyes.

I was fuming as we rode in the car. I didn't speak a word to Gbenga. I was hurt and embarrassed at the same time. All I could do was sit in the back of the car tracing tiny rings on the boys' scalp and pulling on their ears as I held them tight. We pulled up to the office just as Phillip and Bola, two staff, returned to the office. It was two o'clock, they must have been coming from making a deposit at the bank.

"E.D.! You na fine oh, how you dey?" Bola asked as she hugged me. I laughed as I remembered the staff called me E.D., short for Executive Director.

"Come on," Gbenga said, opening the rear car door and sliding his hand around my shoulders. Steven held loosely onto my other hand. "My momma's back!" he shouted, grinning and pleased with himself and the confidence in his declaration.

I followed Gbenga into the office, anxious to see if anything changed. The first thing I noticed was the way his arm dropped off my shoulder as soon as we hit the lobby. My eyes swept over the office to see Dania standing at the top of the steps with a tear streaming down her face. Her hair was gelled into a slick black mane, her frame tall and thin draped in a long linen skirt and white ruffled blouse.

"Oh, Mommy, *ju* are home, so good to see *ju*, Kimmy." Her thick Spanish tone and swinging hand gestures whisked my traces of anger away. I missed hearing those rolling r's and feeling her cheerful spirit. I had asked Gbenga to hire her as a receptionist before I left. Her husband had lost his job. They had four children at home, and without money coming into the house she would send the children to live with their grandmother back in the Dominican Republic. "*Ju* look fresh," she murmured, voice dissolving before finishing her thought. We were ready to greet with a hug when Gbenga called Dania into his office, brows furrowed, pulling the door closed behind him. The hallway opened into a communal meeting space. Curious, I went into the joining office and held the door while standing in the entry.

"*Shairman*, I am very excited to see *jour* wife has returned home" she said, giving a mild sniffle.

"Yes, she came home and I want to do all I can to make sure she is happy and that I have a fighting chance to show her things have changed."

"I know *ju* are happy to see her home. *Ju* are a beautiful family."

"Yes, my family is whole again, and I want it to stay that way. I do not need any gossip to spoil it." His tone short and brisk.

"*Shairman*?"

"You do not have to call me Chairman. I still do not know who helped my wife to leave the country, but I know you must have spoken to her and none of you Wives put a stop to it. I see the way you whisper. I am also aware of the words you had with Amaka. What I do is not your concern."

"*Ju* are correct, none of *jour* duties are my concern." Dania's honeyed voice became a stern whisper. "I work here because *ju* asked me. I am not *jour* wife or *jour* house girl to speak to any kind of way. I have a husband. I could never think of getting inside of *jour* business. I will also not sit around and be still while some small useless girl uses any opporjunity to push find way into *jour* life and into *jour* bed. I never said a word to Mrs. Ndili about Amaka. It only became obvious when Amaka would find reasons necessary to carry work for *ju* down to *jour* house, often times not coming back to *de* office at all!"

"Your assumptions make you a risk, and I will not risk losing my wife."

"*Jour* reaction makes tis a joke, and I quit!"

I stood in the doorway with knots in my stomach, surprise surging in my chest. Gbenga was always adamant about other people respecting me. I don't know what threw me, the conformation of what I expected or the way God chose to reveal it to me. I held onto the door frame, reflecting on the conversations in Igbo that would be cut short when I entered the room and the plastic smiles Amaka would give me as she would walk away. The way she gazed at him when he came into the office, staring as if his bold colored neck tie was pointing down at his penis. She would powder her smooth cocoa skin, adjust her breasts in her cotton blouse and improve her posture at her desk. I knew. The same way I knew he was having an affair in Houston with someone in Florida. The trips to New York when he said he was shopping for me. The nights he would travel promoting Reggae shows or hanging out with the guys. Or the time he would pick arguments, just to go "cool off."

Then, as if to just fall in my lap, he sends me to our storage to find a book. Inside a luggage, underneath dozens of books I run across pictures of him and her, a beautiful, slender young girl with toffee skin and short curly hair pouncing around on the beach with my husband. I remember the look in his eyes, the half smile he flashes trying to keep me off balance, telling me it was an old picture. Idiot! He forgot he was wearing the bracelet I bought him only months before, or the fact the photo following it showed the two of them at the Superbowl. The roman numerals on the huge marquee in the background gave it away. My feelings then and even now were mixed: if he wanted someone else, why wouldn't he let me out? Why the lies? Why was he always bringing me back? The little arguments with me must have made him feel justified to cheat. I often wondered how a woman who appeared so bright had no idea he had a wife. Maybe she didn't, but Amaka did.

"Mommy, are you up here?" Malcolm darted around the corner calling out my name.

I stood frozen, wondering if Gbenga heard him. I quickly burst into the bathroom, closing the door and turning the handle on the faucet.

"Malcolm, I am in the restroom. I will be out in a moment." I stood over the sink, shaking my head in the mirror, thoughts flying weightless, like artificial snowflakes after shaking a glass snow ball. I didn't even want to look at him right now. "Gbenga, I am going to have Mr. Mathew drop the boys and me at home. See you later."

Later that evening Gbenga came in the den smiling, sat down, and pulled me to sit beside him. "I'm sorry about today. When you left I didn't know if you would have someone come to the school and take the boys, so I had to tell the school to be cautious. I couldn't stand to lose them too." He held my gaze, and kissed me so gently I felt my resistance shatter like glass. The rhythm of his voice was like an old school slow jam calming the restless fear I associated with Gbenga's softest touch. "I am going to put this family back together," he said, eyes bright, "and I am going to start by showing you how much I love you." He lifted my feet slowly and undid the straps on my sandals and eased each one off. We fell into an easy silence. He wrapped a blanket around me and led me out to the love seat on our balcony. The faint breeze of the ocean moved the hot air over me. I sat quietly, not wanting words to get in the way of what I was feeling.

For months I was open to a fresh start and tried to keep everything smooth at home. I studied his movements, his scent; more frankincense than sandalwood, memorizing over fifteen ways he could wrinkle his eyes and what each one of them meant. I was careful to not even mention anything about going to work, but I knew extra money coming into the house meant taking some pressure off of him. I could feel he was making efforts too. Each night he would ask me if I prayed for us, and he would hold me tight, as if he thought I might get up and leave. Some mornings he would have Esther bring blooms of ginger and birds of paradise to place next to my bed in the morning with simple notes: "Malaika," my angel, "Can't wait to see you," "Always us." We went regularly to the Ikoyi Club as a family. He had custom frames made for all of our family pictures, and he hung every one. Seeing the joy on the boys' faces was becoming a turn-on for me. The more love he showed them, the more love I wanted to give him. I saw family time as the two and three of our foreplay.

Kinder Binder

I woke in the morning to drive to the market.

"Esther, call the driver. We need to get some things from the market."

"He is outside washing the car, Ma. Oga says he will be driving with you today."

My husband rarely went to the market with me, especially Mile Twelve, and depending on the circumstance, he would rather call his sister to go with me. The markets are crowded and frenzied, but somehow functional. It struck me as odd, but maybe it was part of the new him. I motioned towards the rear door.

"I'm going to ride. I want to buy some fish from under the bridge." Gbenga remarked as he opened the door for me.

"The boys would love some shrimp too." I grabbed my empty bags and sat in the car.

Arriving at Mile Twelve we came down from the car. A young boy wearing an oversized shirt and rolled-up denims came to greet us. He asked if we needed a guide around. I handed him my list and asked him to help us find everything and carry it back to our car. We walked very briskly for an hour, through the narrow maze of produce, examining skins of everything from banana, to tomatoes, yam, apples, corn, melon and oranges. I nearly choked as we walked through rows and rows of fresh onion and dried peppers sitting in the sun. Men were crouched like kids playing jacks as they cut fresh meat against wooden boards while blaring out first and last prices.

"Why don't you just send Esther and the driver to the market?" Gbenga balked.

"I love coming here. It's Nigeria. I love the people, I love the bartering, it's exhilarating!"

After we packed the bags and baskets in the trunk, I tipped the boy and got in the car.

"Mathew, stop under the bridge before reaching home so we can get some fish." I grinned as I took some money out of my bra and placed it back in my purse.

"I want to stop by the cyber café on our way back to Victoria Island," Gbenga instructed.

We drove on Ozumba Mbadiwe Street pulling up near the Proflex Gym. It was Saturday, and the small strip center was bustling with activity. "I will run into Cactus to get some desserts for dinner tomorrow," I said, pointing to the restaurant next door. "What do you have a taste for?"

"It's better to choose when you see them displayed at the counter. I will go in with you as soon as we finish here," Gbenga gestured, holding his hand out to me. "Come with me. It will only take a second."

We entered the café, stopping briefly to pay the attendant for 15 minutes of internet time. She handed him a small piece of paper. Gbenga guided me forward, his hand lightly touching my back.

"Pull up your email account."

"What do you mean?" I asked, blood percolating like a pot of hot coffee.

"I want you to open up your yahoo account. We are starting from the truth, so there should be nothing to hide. Open up your emails!" His commands seemed to echo in the small café.

My mind was racing; I didn't think anything would be there, because for months since my return I hadn't thought about emailing anyone. I stared at the screen intently, wondering if any of the gigabytes would bite me later. Inbox: twenty-three new emails.

"Move over and let me see." Gbenga demanded.

"Go ahead, Gbenga, open it up yourself. This is ridiculous! I don't have anything to hide." I got up from my position, placing a chair between us before I sat down.

"Hmff, okay, mmmmm," Click! His fingers tapped away at the keys. "Nothing to hide eh? Then what is this bullshit?"

I moved closer to read the mail:

I have been waiting for weeks to talk to you. I want to call you often, but thought my son's voice in the background may make you sad. I wanted to give you time, but thoughts of you keep jumping around in my head. I went to Stacy's house, but she told me you went back to Nigeria. I hope you are careful. Please call me to let me know you are safe. Our time together was special. You are always on my mind. –Scott

"Scott! Who the fuck is Scott?" his gaze became narrow, as he bit his lip.

My body became stiff and my stomach iced over. "You've met him. He used to come in to the restaurant," my eyes refusing to blink. "We have some mutual friends."

"Call him! Call him right now!"

I flinched. "I don't have his number."

"Sit down right here and type him a message," he grabbed the back of the chair and slammed it in front of the computer station.

"What am I typing?"

Gbenga bent over, leaning into my ear. I could tell his nostrils were still flared as his breath fell heavy with every consonant in the words he spoke. "Write that you are back in Nigeria. You have been thinking about the last time he touched you and the way you made love!"

"We did NOT make love!" I turned, one eye squinting, facing him in the chair. "I am not writing that. It didn't happen!"

"We'll see," he smirked, with the amused twist of his lips.

"You know what you are looking for. You type the message! While you are at it, write down my username and password to my account. I don't have anything to hide." The flippin' nerve! I got up, pushing the chair back with my legs. "I am trying to make this work. I am here, with YOU!" I scribbled my username and password on the piece of paper and walked out the door.

In a moment's time, Gbenga came to the car muffling instructions to Mathew. We drove back across the IBB Bridge, to a two-story building off Surulere Street. I hesitated to get out of the car. I had missed the sign board before we pulled in. A young woman sat in a wheelchair out front, as a nurse came from behind, dressed in a white uniform and carrying a small brown paper bag.

"Come inside with me while I speak to the doctor."

"Is this Dr. Hassan's clinic? " I asked, moving cautiously as we walked inside, passing an older man with hand wrapped in bloody bandages.

Gbenga was speaking on the phone as a tall, wiry, dark-skinned man wearing a stethoscope reached to take his hand. Abruptly Gbenga placed his phone in his pocket and grasped the man's hand with both of his, holding on with familiarity. As they spoke, the man looked over at me and I nodded. The two of them walked towards me, the doctor making broad gestures with his hands.

"So, you would like to try one more time for a baby girl, is it?" The man spoke with a wide, toothed grin.

My voice lodged on the flat of my tongue. "We spoke about it once or twice, quite a while ago."

"Kim, this is Dr. Coker, he and his wife own this clinic." Gbenga interjected, reaching for my hand.

"Nice to meet you," I replied, anxious for an explanation.

"My wife Rosario and I met while at med school in Cuba. She is a Nigerwife, you may know her," he questioned, as we followed him down the hallway.

"I'm not sure. I know a few families named Coker."

My thought was interrupted as we passed through a pair of double doors labeled- BIRTHING ROOM. The sound of curtain rings running across the metal rod broke my daze.

"Go ahead and get comfortable" the doctor requested.

Comfort was contrary to what I was feeling. "Gbenga?"

"Let the doctor look and make sure everything is all right. I'm right here. I will not leave your side," he spoke, as he took my purse from off my shoulder, wrapped his arm behind my back, and helped me onto the table. I lay on the cold table, the tissue paper rumpling beneath my shaking legs.

"You will be more comfortable if you put your legs in the stirrups," he said, dismissing the sandals that were still on my feet.

I glanced over at Gbenga. "Do not do this, please." My voice was dissolving before I could finish my thoughts.

Gbenga stepped forward as the doctor reached to pull the privacy curtain, his eyes glaring as I lay on the table.

"You are going to have to remove your panties, and sit back on the table," instructed the doctor.

Gbenga stood, his strong silhouette looking over me. His silence has never been more terrifying, nor spoken more deafening. He didn't utter a word or move a muscle.

I closed my eyes real tight, squeezing my lids, trying to make my body below my waist go away. I had to do it slowly, until the creases in my eyelids rolled over each other. My toes went first, one after the other, then my knees, but traveling up my thighs takes slow rhythmic breaths to push the numbness further. I tried to lie still pushing my back deeper into the examining table, coming up on my elbows and tearing the tissue paper beneath my hands. I could feel the pull against the walls of my cervix, scraping, stinging and tearing of wet tissue. I sucked my breath until my tongue vibrated against the nubby roof of my mouth and the release made a hissing sound. My eyes flew open with misery as the last fleshy part of my vagina released the IUD, setting bloody between my legs. I clenched my knees together and lay back on the table. I felt a bare hand on my knee, soon after a jolt of lightening straightened my spine as I suffered the singe of a bare finger jabbing inside of me. My stomach and womb collapsed, hurling into each other as I spilled onto the floor.

"Enough! Damn, enough! How dare you touch me, Gbenga. You can't make a baby with a corpse!" I protested, less concerned about what germs I may have been exposed to dragging my bare ass across the clinic floor.

"I need to be sure there is nothing else you are hiding blocking our efforts to conceive."

His words sounded cold and clinical. Making babies meant making love and I was feeling no love right now. At that moment, a tall, slender woman wearing a knee length khaki skirt and a white medical jacket embroidered "Dr. Coker" walked into the room. She smelled faintly of hairspray, her dark wavy hair pulled back and finished with a large blue clip-on bow around the bun. She had exotic features, distinctive cheek bones, full lips and unblemished bronze-toned skin. "I can check her. You cannot just put your hands anyhow after such a procedure. You could risk infection," she interjected sympathetically, supporting my arm as she pulled me from the floor.

"How could you do this to me, Gbenga? How could you do it like this?" I ranted, disgusted as I saw the smudge of blood that ran from the examining table to the floor. The muscles around my womb groaned, breath dragging through my throat.

"Me? How could you do this to me? How could you not tell me you were using birth control?"

"I spoke to you about not being ready. I did not want to bring…" I looked at Dr. Coker and quickly closed my mouth. As the pain intensified and shot up through my pelvis, it was a habit to cover up our dirty little problems.

"You are a liar! A god-damned liar! That's the only thing you are good at." His chest heaved and I could see his pain. He wanted so much to have another child. He wanted to give me the baby girl I dreamed of.

I thought, I have never feared anyone enough to lie, him included. But Lord, I have lied to keep from seeing. "Yes, I am a liar. I lie so well I have convinced myself. You can identify it, because you have asked me to do it to cover for you so damn often. I lied in the States about your lifestyle. I have lied for years about the bruises, and most of all I lied every damn time I thought we would be different!"

I dressed, not concerned with discretion, leaving the sanitary napkins sitting on the counter and feeling the twisted elastic at my waist from my panties. I ran to the car, slamming the door with all of the strength in me as the driver stared and said nothing. He opened the door for Gbenga, got in, and uninvolved drove us home.

I scrambled out of the car, stomach fluttering with nausea. I heard the boys inside mocking their favorite wrestlers on the television. All I could think of was soaking in some hot water. I kissed the boys quickly and toddled up to my room. I walked into the bathroom, flipped the switch to the water heater, and noticed blood soaking through my skirt. I leaned down to pull it off as Gbenga pulled me up from my elbow, our eyes within inches, staring back at each other.

Through the years of fights I have screamed, I have cowered, and a few times I felt I blocked enough to get a few good licks in myself. This time, I did something I hadn't done in the dozen times this had happened. I stood up, ran towards him and cried, "Is that it?" I grunted, my chest heaving for air. "Is that all you have?"

He rounded me so quickly my spit and my words couldn't catch up with my mouth. Snatching me to turn around, he had his nine milli in one hand and a fist full of my hair in the other. Like a puppet master he manipulated my every move. "Did you fuck him? Did you?" Stretching the skin on my cheeks beneath his thumb and pointer finger, I couldn't move my jaw, only my lips.

He was firing questions and insults at me as fast as I imagined it would take a bullet from the gun to rip through my flesh. I could admit to myself, if no one else, that I wanted to know the feeling of being in his arms. Not the same way or depth I wanted endless love from Gbenga, but just as real.

"No Gbenga, no!" I wheezed, trying to twist my shoulders in line with my neck.

"Slut, I will kill you if you give my pussy away. Kill you, dead!" He jerked my head, pulling my hair, burning my scalp like embers and throwing me heavily to the floor. "This never would have happened if you hadn't left," he said, and even as I crawled away from him I could feel his shoes kicking at my sides, his arms wailing at my shoulders and the butt of the gun catching me on the side of my face.

There was stillness and I opened my eyes. I turned my head to see him sitting on the edge of the bed, head lowered, tears rolling, holding the gun to his chest. "You gave up on me. There are people burying charms on my property, stealing my money, and plotting for my downfall, but you want to take away my heart. I can't live without my heart."

I pulled myself to his feet. Blood dripped on his toes as moved the trunk of my body upright. I rested my hand on his foot, massaging slowly in between his toes, as I did during much happier times, only this time it was blood and not baby oil. "Look at me, I'm here. I am right here. Put it down and hold me. We'll get through this." I moved up the side of his leg, only turning my head to rest on his knee, eyebrows stretching to keep my eyes peeled on the gun.

He sat, still bent over, stony-eyed, digging the gun deeper into his chest. "The hurting is going to stop tonight, I'll make it stop." I could feel his tears landing delicately on the top of my head. It wasn't only me he was fighting. He was fighting his own demons.

"We don't need to hurt each other. Let's try loving each other. What about the boys, baby?"

I spoke cautiously, holding his eyes with my gaze, and I saw something in his piercing eyes that few people ever had- a quiet desperation. He lowered the gun and set it on the bed. It took me a minute to shake myself out of my daze, letting all the words I wanted to say clutter the space in my head.

I had only remembered seeing Gbenga cry once. It was August of 1997, when he received the news his icon, Fela had died. It was an odd feeling, like seeing a lion carrying a baby antelope to safety between his enormous sharp teeth. When I pictured Gbenga, I never pictured him with his mouth foaming, pupils dilated, and standing over top of my broken body waving his fists. I had always pictured him with his hands wrapped gently around my waist, supporting me from behind while watching our boys play on the beach. I saw him grilling fresh fish in the back yard as I looked out from the balcony of the beautiful mansion that we designed together in his village, as the boys splashed in the pool. He was the man who talked about building Black nations, and leaving legacies to his grandchildren. This to me was Gbenga, and that was who I wanted to grow old with. Even in the very worst times, I never saw myself as weak. I identified myself as humble. I never thought less of myself, I just thought about myself less. I saw the strength in unconditional love, an example of someone who would stick and stay. I understood that marriages take work, and no one would ever fill everything you desired. If they did, what would you need God for? Selfish people were the weak ones. They couldn't see past themselves. But to forgive shows humility. Forgiveness is tough; it takes a strong person to forgive. I wasn't interested and didn't see myself as a victim. I was a fighter, a conqueror, and love conquers all, right?

Morning greeted me. I rolled over to find his side of the bed pulled up with the pillows fluffed and propped up on the headboard. I shook my head and ran my fingers through my hair, hoping I had just awakened from a dream. I sat up with sharp pangs as I extended my back. The windows and balcony door were open. I heard the ocean and the birds, but the sound seemed to be on low. I lowered my shoulders and stretched my neck back, but a throbbing pain lured my head back down to the pillow.

"Madam, madam," there was a tap at the bedroom door. "Madam, you don wake?"

"Yes, Esther, I de wake." Pulling my robe across my body, I gingerly walked to the bathroom.

"Madam, your breakfast is here. Can I get you anything?"

"Where are the boys? Have they gone to school?"

"No madam, they are with their aunty Ufoma. She took them to Chocolate Royal."

"Ok, thank you, I will be down in a minute. Could you please make me some tea?" I pulled a washcloth out of the cabinet and held it under the water. I covered my face, taking the brisk chill into my pores. The skin around my left eye felt tight as the tension chewed on my temple. I straightened up from leaning over the bowl, took the cloth from my face and saw that freakish bump growing on the side of my face was not a dream- it was a damn nightmare. I got in the shower, dressed, grabbed some plantain, wrapped my head with a head tie, and walked downstairs to the balcony off the den. It was still early in the day. I could see the fishermen's canoes, buoyed like seagulls, their nets cast and stretched like wings. I wasn't ready to see anyone. I just wanted to walk.

I looked into the Atlantic Ocean recollecting my own life. I was floundering in an ocean of frustration and confusion and I needed a lifeline. Gbenga's angry words rolled over me like waves coming in from the ocean; some crashed and broke, moving pieces and pulling them deep into the water;

others arch and flow, mixing in with the rest of the landscape, the volume is unpredictable, but you know they are coming. I remember Grandma saying: "Whatever your heart is full of, it will overflow out of your mouth." All I remembered from Gbenga anymore was hurtful, hateful towards me and bouts of silent weeping. His tongue seemed to work all by itself, with no help from his mind. How could I kiss his lips or meet his tongue when I knew there's venom seeping from his throat? When I talked it wasn't anything he wanted to hear and if I didn't talk I must have been up to something. Like an addiction, it was getting longer and further from the highs I used to feel when I was with him. The sun slashed against my arms, but the sky is always gray through black and blue eyes. I walked past the water tower and onto the beach, stepping and praying as if I had psalms in the lining of my belly. I called out to my grandmother in heaven and asked her to watch over me.

"God, grant the guardian angels you assigned to keep watch over me."

I paced my way up the steps of the house. I glanced as I saw Malcolm's dusty socks kicked up on the sofa. Coming closer I pinched his big toe, expecting him to squirm, but he didn't budge. Paying closer attention, I noticed he was holding a Harry Potter book in front of his face but it was turned upside down.

"I see you are almost finished with your new book. You get faster each time you read. Do you like this one?"

"Um-hmm." He responded, voice shaken.

"Well baby, you can't read very fast with the book upside down," I said, as I softly pushed the hard cover down towards his chest, revealing his tear-soaked cheeks. "What is it, Malcolm?"

"I'm o.k" he said, turning his hands over on each other.

"Something is bothering you, honey. Let me know so I can fix it," I responded, taking my seat next to him and brushing away his tears.

"He broke his word. I hate him! He broke his word!"

"Baby, you don't hate your dad. I don't hate your dad. It took the love from two of us to make one incredible you, and I thank God everyday for that."

"Hmm, thank God." He nodded, with a look of almost adult understanding.

I turned to walk up the steps to my bedroom, when Malcolm's haste to go downstairs caught my attention. Maybe what he said in our conversation made me a little itchier than usual. No, that wasn't right. I wasn't itchy at all...not about his words anyway. It was just a feeling in my stomach, lingering…what? I abruptly stopped without calling him, removed my slippers, tip toeing, so he wouldn't hear my steps walking down the stairs. I heard the sounds of the cabinets being opened and closed in the kitchen. He was immersed in finding something in the cabinet. He could have wanted a snack or a bowl of cereal. No, it wasn't that, because he knew the cereal was in the larger cupboard next to the refrigerator. I stood, tracing the cause of cool air feeling on my neck and shoulders. Malcolm stood on his tip toes, reaching and stretching his fingers to the top of the cabinet. When his hand emerged he was holding his father's favorite glass in his hand.

It was a tall earthenware tiki cup he had since our very first date at Kahiki Supper Club on East Broad Street. Gbenga always drank from this cup every evening. It was taller than most of the glasses in the cabinet and held a significant amount of ice, but its distinction clearly made it preferred. Malcolm placed it on the counter, turning around with slow curiosity. I pulled my head back from the door, waiting for a noise to signal more investigation. My mind wondered if he was going to destroy the cup somehow. I listened, but I didn't hear breaking of glass, instead I heard a steady decreasing tone from liquid bouncing off the contents filling the glass. I poked my head around the corner, my eyebrows ready to run from my face. Malcolm seemed angered to have it pour so carelessly from the mouth of the container.

Tiny pieces of rat poison fell onto the counter, followed by a quick shot of drain opener. He topped it off by running fresh pineapple through the juicer, another one of his dad's favorites, and filling the frothy yellow fluid to the rim. He turned to open the refrigerator door, tenderly grasping the cup with both tiny hands and placing it inside.

Panic filled my eyes, I crouched behind the dining table, my head bowed into my knees as thoughts and sadness ricocheted around my mind. I heard his padded footsteps scurry back up the steps greeted by his brother; "let's play Spiderman bro!"

I sprang to the kitchen, flung open the door to the fridge, grabbed the cup and flung all of the contents into the sink. A few days ago I might have sat

Malcolm down and talked to him about his anger. Years from now I might. At this moment, I couldn't find the words to say or the questions to ask. I gazed at the liquid as it made its way down the drain, and tried to keep the corners of my eye dry. Turning on water as hot as I could stand, I scorched and sponged every groove of the cup until I was interrupted by a turn of the key at the back door.

"Madam, would you like me to wash the cup for you?" Esther asked as she closed the door behind.

"No," I replied, giving one final rinse filling it partially with water and taking a sip. "I want you to juice some pineapple and mango and leave this for my husband to have with dinner." I took one more drink and swallowed hard, feeling nothing but warm liquid down the back of my throat.

Later that evening, the boys and I ate dinner, as they told me what happened on the latest episode of Dragon Ball Z. Animated faces and energetic sound effects rounded the table between bites and chews of jollof rice and chicken. Malcolm would start to tell me about a scene and Steven would finish his sentence followed by a chorus of "Mom, you should have seen it."

At dinner, the vegetable soup and jollof rice having relaxed his mood, Gbenga picked up the chat we'd begun while the boys and I were at the table.

"Is this show on every day?" Gbenga asked, as he swallowed a finger full of fufu.

"Every day! Well, maybe not Sunday." Steven grabbed the leg of the drumstick and put it in his mouth.

"Esther, bring me the juice I saw in the refrigerator."

Malcolm forked his plantains on top of his jollof rice. I got so consumed with watching Malcolm, I dropped some rice off my spoon into my cup, where it waded to the bottom.

He never took his eyes off his dad; he sized up his father the way a boxer does his challenger. Gbenga didn't notice Malcolm had stopped talking. Esther washed her hands before going into the refrigerator. Gbenga was dipping his fingers to rinse them in the water bowl at the same time, hollering, "Esther! Bring me the juice and a cup of water."

As she turned away from the refrigerator, hands still slippery from the water, the tiki cup went crashing to the floor.

"Foolish girl!" Gbenga shouted.

"Idiot!" Malcolm balked.

"I'm sorry sir." Esther sheepishly replied.

"Malcolm, apologize to Esther. It was a mistake," I directed. I'm sure he wanted to choose bigger words, but his young vocabulary kept him from being too colorful. My mind was at ease and praising God. His plan was better than mine.

"He doesn't need to apologize," Gbenga interrupted, "it is the truth." He looked at Malcolm tapping him on the arm as he got up from the table.

"Hmm, if you only knew" my mind reflected, "If you only knew."

Back to the peacefulness of the morning, Malcolm was less angry during breakfast, but still guarded. I had tossed and turned through the night, reflecting on the amount of pain and damage he must have felt to want to hurt his father. I sat on the bathroom floor, reduced to frenzied prayers. I wanted to fix this. I loaded up the Range Rover for a luncheon at the beach.

We rode through Lekki Peninsula as Malcolm sat, void of expression looking out the window. Steven was perched on the edge of the backseat challenging his seat belt when he asked, "Dad, how do brown cows that eat green grass make white milk?"

"Everyone knows brown cows make chocolate milk."

"Nu-uh daddy, Malcolm told me all cows make white milk, goats too."

I looked over my shoulder at Malcolm. Usually he is the one with the quickest wit, but he sat still, pushed back into the seat. A lanky young boy in cut off jeans ran alongside the car as we turned onto the service road to the beach. "Park here oga! You dey park?" he called out, running out of his flip flops. Malcolm didn't flinch. He would normally engage them by bantering back and forth in broken English. It was as if he wouldn't allow himself to be fun. The water was my way to his funny bone. We found a spot between rows of palm trees. As we were coming down from the Range, Malcolm had his hands full and I smothered his cheeks with kisses.

Malcolm soon pepped up, challenging me to a race at the edge of the sand.

"I almost caught a crab, daddy," Steven called, eyes beaming.

Gbenga sat back while reading in the rattan lounger. "Keep tryin'," the newspaper answered.

I walked over to Gbenga and handed him a mango. "Malcolm has been playing football with the boys from the beach. He's really trying to get better. He hasn't had much of an opportunity to watch you play. Why don't you go show him just how good his daddy can play?" I winked and rolled the ball around to his feet.

Good, I thought. Maybe Malcolm could get over his anger with his dad, his superman since the time he collected his first action figure. Malcolm admired his dad. I always felt he learned to walk early, just so he could keep up with his daddy's every move. His eyes lit up when Gbenga addressed him as "my boy", and you could almost see the wind let out of him if Gbenga introduced him as Malcolm. I could be with the boys all day; playing and laughing, but when daddy came home, they competed for his affections. Lately, they refer to him as the "fun-sucker". Gbenga rarely meets his son's eyes and answers their chirpy questions with monosyllables. Back in the day, Gbenga would recite poetry and bedtime stories that would make me turn off the television, so I could hear them in the room. He exposed Malcolm to reggae, jazz and world music, and probably to things I will never know about during jeep rides and trips to the mall. There is no easier way to learn than through personal experience. And no impressions are more engrained than the ones which run through your blood.

The boys kicked the ball back and forth with their father for nearly an hour. Steven fell out next to me under the umbrella, energy drained from the sun. Gbenga was spent, twisting his shirt into a sandy wet wad around his neck.

Malcolm caught a second wind and jumped in the waves one last time before settling to grab a fist full of foil wrapped smoked turkey leg from the basket.

The sun pinched the creases in my sleepy eyes, as they tightened with a yawn. The hot rays always brightened my mood, while the water cleared my head. Sometimes I wish we had built our "vacation" house next to the ocean first, instead of the concentrating all of our efforts to the house in the village. But, many Igbos still suffer from the post-Biafran syndrome. A particular kind of intergenerational trauma carried after the Nigerian civil war. Igbo people were extremely resilient during the war when they were cut off from the rest of the country, and as a result they felt security only lied within the perimeters of their villages.

We loaded up to go home. Malcolm and Steven laughed and talked in the back seat. I reached back to squeeze Malcolm's leg and grinned.

Arriving home, Malcolm, Steven and I stretched out sideways on the bed. Gbenga joined to lay close behind. There was stillness. I laid there staring at the ceiling—visualizing the couple running hand in hand on the beach smiling, water lapping at the tips of our toes. The quiet and mushiness was too much for the boys, or maybe they wanted to let us have time to ourselves. Steven turned to kiss me before they dashed off the bed and out the door.

"I-I--" my voice broke, "I like us like this, I just want you to hold onto me." The simple gesture of me asking made him let out a sigh. He moved closer, folding me into his arms, spooning me, his breath moving the hairs on my head. I was frozen, drinking him in.

Slip Knot

Gbenga was in his element talking politics, music and culture to such a diverse group of friends. He's a man of diverse intellectual sophistication. The four of them sat on the balcony drinking stout, eating grilled fish, talking current events and ranting over recent election fiascos. His conversations were spiced with quotes from Marcus Garvey to Socrates. When talking about Nigeria he always spoke with obsessive zeal, reading on the internet or scouring This Day newspaper until he could speak about current events with the flair and mastery of a CNN analyst.

Imagine watching ABC's The View sub-Saharan edition with all of the quick wit and varied personalities; Three Nigerians and one African American, discussing Nigeria's first sustained transition from one civilian government to another. Scores of people were injured or dead at the hands of supporters and members of the top two political parties; People's Democratic Party and Alliance for Democracy. All of them were disgusted over the declaration from President Obasango regarding the "peaceful election process" and the lack of international response to human rights violations. Gbenga "Walters" led the topics. His focused drive and singular devotion to his countrymen made for interesting moderating, so did endless beers and bottles of wine.

I peeked out at the patio table to see many of the bottles were empty. "Can I get anyone something else to drink?"

"We're good, thanks Kim," answered by nodding heads and flashes of teeth. Being cautious about not looking directly in the eyes of a man had become a habit over the years.

"Maybe we'll take some more food to settle the stout," Gbenga requested, scooting the table forward so he could pass by. "I'll be right back."

I went to the kitchen to grab some beers out of the fridge. I heard footsteps descending the stairs. I closed the door and was startled by Maduka standing motionless right in front of me. He was tall and wiry, russet brown with a strong jaw and mouth full of big white teeth smiling back at me.

"Kim, I have wanted to tell you I am sorry for not paying attention to what had happened to you the last time you left for the States. I don't think a man should put his hands on a woman ever and I had no idea Gbenga was hitting you. Gbenga is my man. We have been friends for a very long time. He is a good businessman with excellent instincts and an innate sense of enterprise, like no one I have ever seen. He made owning a filling station sexy. But, I have known you since you lived in Houston, you are my sister. I will help you if I can, you do not deserve to be hit on, however I will not help you take the boys from him. The boys are Nigerians. They need to be here with their father."

I stood expressionless, the way you get when you receive a complement and someone takes it away in the same breathe. "I appreciate the sentiment, but the boys are ours, not his. They need to be where they will be nurtured. Hopefully Gbenga and I won't have reason to make those choices. Thanks for caring though." I placed the beers on the tray to walk them upstairs.

I got to the first landing and Melvin was on his way down. "Kim, where is the bathroom? I think Gbenga is in the one upstairs."

"Oh, just go to the bottom of the steps to the right of the door," I motioned with my elbow. You'll see a bathroom there."

"Here I can take that," he said, reaching for the tray of drinks. "Does everyone have these trays at home?"

"What trays?"

"You know, every time you go to a wedding, a birthday or a funeral Nigerians are always giving out Tupperware with someone's name and face all over it." We laughed.

Melvin was my girlfriend Sissy's younger brother from Chicago. He did sales for his brother in-law's petroleum company. He always had a great sense of humor, which was a quality to hold on to when navigating through the shark infested waters of Nigerian business. I didn't know him well. I would occasionally see him at the American embassy events, often times with different girls on his arm. He seemed like a player, but his comedy and chivalry made him stand out in a backdrop of pomp and stature. I handed Melvin the tray. "Thanks." As his body away from the steps, my eyes met Gbenga's intense glare staring down at me from the top of the landing.

I planted myself within earshot, monitoring my husband's face, anxious to gauge his reaction, the key to decoding his mood. His expression remained inscrutable. The group continued drinking between laughs and conversation. The night drug on and I put the boys to sleep. Esther left the house for the evening. I went to the kitchen and make some snacks to help neutralize the effects of the alcohol. As I was looking through the cupboards I heard uneven stutter steps coming down the marble stairs. This normally confident, assured man was drunk, angry and out of control. "I wanted ube, not snails!" Gbenga snarled. "That's your problem, you don't listen."

"Some of the pears were spoiled and hard. There wasn't enough to roast for you and company. I am going to fry some snails in tomato, pepper, and onion or I can make some oil bean with roasted yam," I explained, as the thick orangish-red palm oil dropped like ketchup into the skillet. "Which one sounds better?" I turned to finish cutting the onion as the oil slowly melted across the surface of the pan. I couldn't understand why this was such a big deal. Gbenga ate either choice several times a week.

"I'm sure you can tell me which one sounds better to Melvin," he mocked, slowly taking small steps closer to me. "You seem to know what makes him smile."

Gbenga peered into my face, daring me to search for an answer. I blurted, "Is it the fact you don't know what I was laughing about or the assumption I was laughing without you?"

"He wants you!" he shot back.

The oil started to smoke, as a pungent smell rose from the frying pan. "We talk about the similarities and differences in cultures. Some things are funny and he can relate to them as another African American. The fact Nigerians call us White because we are from America-that is funny. If you felt this way about him-or about me, why did you invite him to our house?"

Gbenga turns with Matrix-like movement, grabbing the pan and slinging the carmelized contents and scorching palm oil onto my back. Pieces of onion and diced tomato were clinging to the linen on my blouse. My stomach heaved. I was certain the skin was sliding off of my back. An excruciating pain caused my muscles to tense and my body to crumble to the ground. My mouth became dry as my body instantly broke into a sweat. My jaw opened before the sound registered-"AHHHHHH!"

I yelled, the crescendo competing with the rumble echoing from nearby generators.

"My house," he raged, with that weird light in his eyes, tossing the pan as it clattered on the stove top. "You can go off with Melvin!"

"There is nothing going on." I responded through gritted teeth. Unsure of what exactly he wanted to hear to feel some security. I laid there, palms spread on the cool marble.

"Go be with him if he makes you happy!" He said, as if my response didn't register.

Fresh tears ran like wax down my cheeks. I thought I'd dissolved, but the nerves in my back were jumping with rage. Gbenga stumbled out of the room. I stood up as straight as I could. I tried to will my body to move, to carry me to the sink. The skin on my back pulled as I arched my back. I felt like my nipples were clamped the floor. All I could think to do was remove my shirt and loosely wrap a beach towel over my shaking shoulders.

When I woke up the next morning, Gbenga's side of the bed was cool and untouched. For a second I stared at the covers, at the neatly placed throw pillows. Normally I wake up to see the ceiling. My eyes were swollen and grainy, I couldn't remember ever waking up to this view. The pillow I used to keep me from rolling over, stuck to the raw skin and pus-like drainage on my back. I couldn't move. It was a Saturday, I think. I had to get up, the boys were home. I just lay on the bed staring at the row of closet doors.

Gbenga sauntered in the room. His eyes scanned over my body. His presence felt like lurking, rather than supportive caress. "I love you," he spoke in a hush. Suddenly the words took on another meaning when I heard them. I laid on the bed staring through his holograph image.

Steven came bouncing in the room with furious speed. I had nothing on from the waist up. I lay still on the bed. "Mommy, you have to get up. It's time for Transformers." His eyes are like a camera lens; clicking shut, then opening to capture each image. "Mommy, what happened?"

"You come back and tell me all about it baby, Mommy isn't feeling too well today, my back hurts, I hurt my back, I mean, I just feel under the weather, but I am ok," painting on a smile. "You and bro watch it and tell me about it when I get up." I made my voice as peppy as I could. Steven kissed my head and walked out of the room. I was becoming a deliberate schizophrenic.

But now, seeing me in obvious visible discomfort changed things. I was in no position to bandage myself. I couldn't reach the pain. He would have to look at it up close. There were blisters on my back. They couldn't be smoothed over without tearing through the skin and leaving scars. His eyes had to be open for his fingers to navigate their way across the burns.

Ufoma delivered a brown paper wrapped package to Gbenga in the afternoon. He pulled a plastic zip-lock bag from inside. With his hand cupped, he pinched a finger full of gray goo which resembled cooked fat trimmed from a juicy steak. The smell was sour, causing me to turn my head and bury my face into my pillow.

"What is that?" I asked, glancing up from the corner of my eye.

"It's snake fat, from a python," Gbenga replied, rubbing it gently across my wounds. "I asked Momma to send some from the village."

Gbenga's head dropped low as he pressed the oily blubber into my skin, being careful not to pull any loose skin or fragile blisters. After days of saline wash and lose bandages it must have worked, the pain subsided and the wounds healed enough to form soft scabs. "This too shall pass," I thought to myself. I wanted to get back to my routine.

Time passed and it was time for Small World; Lagos' premier fundraising gala for all local area non-profits. Each year attendees would mill about the lush green water-side landscape of the Federal Palace Hotel, standing together in small clusters around tables of diverse delicacies and international wines. Various countries were represented at stations manned by embassy personnel who delighted in showcasing their global decorations and bite size 'tasties' throughout the evening. Most of the guests wore international dress or cultural chic fashions, which added to the festive ambiance.

I held an Executive office with the American Women's Club, but recruiting talent for the stage performance was not an issue for them. AWC was full of ex-cheerleaders, pageant participants, aerobics instructors, soccer moms, and women who spent free time on the internet streaming dance numbers from last season's Country Music Awards. Enlisting NigerWives on the entertainment committee was a bit more of a challenge. We came from different cultural backgrounds. Our dance rehearsals were well on their way. Our diverse group agreed jazz was the universal music form symbolic of our hodge-podge of cultures. We laughed and fellowshipped through dance steps in our living room.

After a rehearsal one of my Aunties sent a driver back to the house. I heard him knock at the door. Esther answered and invited him in the house. Gbenga greeted him downstairs and offered him a chair. "My madam left her bag behind and she asked me to come get it." He said, removing his flip flops and hat in the foyer.

"Kim," Gbenga called.

"Yes."

"His madam left her bag. Can you check for it in the living room?"

I saw a large leather shoulder bag lying next to the couch. I picked it up and carried it downstairs. "Here you go. Sorry you had to come all this way. Please tell her I said I enjoyed seeing her today."

"I will," the driver responded, turning slowly towards the front door.

His hesitation made me wonder if I should give him five naira for making the trip. I walked to the den to look for my purse. "Olu," I called.

"Yes, ma."

"Drive safely," I discretely handed him a twenty naira note.

He closed my hand in his. "No ma," he whispered, looking nervously over his shoulder. "My madam wanted me to tell you not to let money be the reason why you can't leave." He handed me a group of thick folded papers.

I was frozen, but the corners of my eyes watered. I stood still and placed the papers inside of the waist line of my skirt. "Thank you," I said and closed the door behind him. I was standing in the foyer alone. I reached for the papers, unfolded them and realized it was a voucher for three tickets on Virgin Airlines. I folded them and put them back in my skirt.

Gbenga leaned back in his leather swivel chair in the study. He was smiling, over steepled fingers while listening to his office manager report the safe delivery of three tankers to the filling station back East. I used to crave that smile. Now, like that pair of Giuseppe boots I thought I had to have, they look good, but they are uncomfortable as hell. Gbenga met my plaintive glare. I wanted to say something. I wanted to tell him there is no room for jealousy in a marriage. That love will make you do things you never plan to do. That the feelings I used to have of butterfly wings in my stomach for him and the fairy-tale which could have been our life sometimes taunts me, riding the breeze like the echo of a name called from a window. I wanted to tell him the pain chewing at my back while I sweat through old dreams and lingering nightmares, cures a love hangover.

But the fragrance of egusi soup came between us. He came closer, reaching for my hand.

"I would give the world to put the love back into your eyes for me."

"My world is inside this house," I said closing my palms together and resting them in front of me.

"I never meant to hurt you. It was the alcohol."

"I know."

"I brought my mother from the village to see about you," he said in exasperation as if he was still a small child. "She wanted to make you soup. She is not very happy with me." His thoughts seemed to trail off and disappear into a mystical hole.

I let that sink in. His words didn't soothe me. I heard a voice inside of me which kept repeating the word-forgiveness, forgiveness, forgiveness. I smiled, my lips closed and walked to the kitchen to greet my mother in-law.

Momma was being entertained by her grandsons when my girlfriend came to pick me up for a cup of tea. "Momma, would you like to come?"

"No, my dear, you go on."

I got in her Benz, with the promise to bring back some sweets for the boys. We were driving over the bridge to her house when I thought came to me.

"Can we stop at the Embassy? I want to see the process for reporting a stolen passport?"

Heather asked the driver to make a turn to the embassy. They dropped me off at the front of the gate. The usually sight of a serpentine line of people requesting for visas was absent. I went to the security gate and handed the uniform gentleman my Ohio driver's license through the glass. "Do you have an appointment?" the tall black man asked, his voice booming through the intercom.

"I am here to see Ms. Cayton about a stolen passport."

He waved his hand for me to pass. I walked through the turnstile and into the building to be buzzed in. I walked up to a small window and was handed three forms to fill out. I sat in the waiting area filling out the forms on a clip board. I glanced up and saw a picture in black and white print: MISSING-- with a picture of a woman's face on it, Ashley Stevens, last seen… When I finished, I handed the young American woman the completed forms with my driver's license, the boy's birth certificates, three previous passport pictures and a photo copy of the first page of my, Malcolm and Steven's passports. I glanced at the list of processing charges on the sign hanging in the waiting room. I had been carrying my license with me in lieu of our passports, which Gbenga kept secured under a cigar humidor on top of our dresser.

"Have the father sign the form, bring it back tomorrow and it will take two days to pick up the passports." Her voice was stoic as she handed me back my documents.

"My husband is in the car. What if I get his signature and bring it right back in?"

"All right, if you can make it back to this window because we close in twenty minutes."

I swiftly took the documents and headed it to the car. The windows were tinted disguising the occupants. I walked over to the other side and appeared to be talking to someone. I returned to embassy security, back to the desk and handed the woman the signed applications. I opened my wallet, fumbling through each tiny slot, until I found the two hundred dollar bills I had folded and wedged between some business cards and a picture of the boys.

"Two days," she said, handing me my change while stamping the forms and closing the blinds across her window.

"Thank you."

If you would have asked me when I woke up that morning would I be going to the American Embassy I would have said no, but there I was.

18 Nailed

Most people don't fear the end of a relationship. It's not the sad part; it's the struggle of knowing how to begin again. The beginning--that's where the fear is. With Gbenga we were always starting over and I was always trying to get back to that place where we began, where I was confirmed and loved. I could think of him as a good bad man or a bad good man. Depending on which direction I wanted to hold onto. I should have taken more responsibility in my direction and a bit less caught up while being held. Being complacent and standing still was only meant to be long enough for me to catch my breath. It is not a destination. I know I have a unique blessing with my name on it, but I have to know who I am—not what other people say I am—or I will never recognize it.

I didn't see the detour. No one told me a wrong turn wasn't always identified with orange cones. I was dreaming, sinking, soothing in a warm dark river of kisses, kisses on necks and shoulders, every kiss a deliberate apology. The harder my shell the deeper he would journey to reach me. Mmm, Gbenga, in this moment I feel safe being lost in you, distracted from pain, wet from love's juices and not from tears, the worrying about the boys, my own desires for a parent's love, all of it is lifted off of me and washed away by the ocean of tender kisses, maybe not for long but for now, and really, where else did I want to be?

Days rolled by as our relationship remained in a holding pattern. Or maybe I remained in a holding pattern as our relationship was rolling by.

Gbenga was cheerful as he packed his clothes for his trip to Abuja. His style was impeccable. Watching him pack for business was a tactical session on the Black Label Art of War. His light blue embroidered caftan was subtle, but he made it look regal. I couldn't stop holding him with my eyes, taking away the soft musk scent of his skin, the timbre of his voice. I briefly fumbled through his bag, making sure he didn't forget his toothbrush, some lotion, or any other necessity out of his toiletry bag. Across the room, Gbenga was adjusting his cufflinks. "Well," I said brightly. "I will go get the boys so you can tell them goodbye."

Gbenga glanced over at me. "Yeah, where are my boys?"

"I can hear them downstairs. Malcolm! Steven, come give daddy a hug." The boys came into the room, still carrying on from the game downstairs. Malcolm hugged his dad with one arm and looped the other arm under the straps of the garment bag. Steven climbed on the bed and lunged into his father's arms, grabbing onto his neck.

"I will be back late tomorrow evening; you guys take care of your Mommy."

"Back in time to watch wrestling?" Steven asked.

"If my flight is not delayed- I will be back in time to watch wrestling." Gbenga answered, gently tossing Steven back onto the bed.

"How about some vegetable soup when you get back?" I slipped my arms around Gbenga, trying to memorize the span of his back, his scent, the degree of tilt to his head when my chin was nestled into his shoulder. I rubbed my cheek against the soft nubby whiskers of his edged goatee, kissing him gently on the cheek. He turns to kiss me, thick, soft lips holding onto mine. I needed these things to cling to when the boys showed anger about their father's neglectfulness. Gbenga responded, by tenderly squeezing me at my waist. I needed that for the times they needed an example of what affection looked like when it was there chance at love. I turned in his arms. "I could fix egusi soup. That would be tasty."

Gbenga smiled. "What would be tasty is some of you when I come home."

"Ok," I laughed. "But you are going to miss some good soup. Your mom showed me a few secrets. I think I've gotten much better."

"Surprise me," Gbenga said, and walked down stairs where the driver was waiting for him.

Riding to work felt different that day. I looked through the crowded faces moving back and forth to work. The day went on as any other. I logged on, pulled my sales sheet out of the folder, and started to send my follow up emails. I wrote my letters for posting and sat with the guys in development to talk about images for university websites. After directing the sales team, reading client requests and updating my folders it was nearly the close of the day before I realized I hadn't eaten.

I went to the bathroom before descending the stairs of my office building. I could see the parishioners dipping their fingers in the holy water outside of the door before entering the beautiful Catholic Church down below. The roundabout was busy with taxis blowing their horns, danfos overloading with passengers, and anxious workers jumping on and off okadas while exchanging dirty naira notes on their trek to go home for the evening. Even at the end of a long day it always amazes me that Lagosians keep their brilliantly colored clothes, traditional and Western, unruffled while scooting through crowded streets and impossibly crowded public transport. My eyes went back to the pristine statue of the Virgin Mary, her face accepting, her arms extended and palms facing upwards. There was a woman kneeling in front of the statue with a long-stem ginger flower in her hand. The flower was bright red, its bloom almost set afire with color. She wore a long shapeless skirt and had a light blue scarf on her head, the edges tenderly flowing on the wind. She did not make the sign of the cross as she stood, placing the flower at the feet of the Virgin. I was touched by the act. Maybe the not knowing her faith was what stood out, or maybe the symbolism of the flower being a torch used to show the way under the comforting eyes of the Virgin Mary. I'm not sure. I'm not even Catholic, but I am a woman about to bear my cross. At that very moment the words moved from my gut and to my head: "Go!"

I sat at my desk, my hands resting on the edge of the black key board. My eyes lifted to the monitor as I typed an address into the toolbar: www.newsalemcares.com. I navigated my way through the website's pages and clicked on "prayer request." I remembered visiting this church the last time I was home, sitting in the balcony as I listened to the sermon. I heard the clack of my nails tapping the keys as I wrote: I am not sure who is going to get this, but I am asking you to pray. I am currently in Nigeria. I have been living in an abusive relationship. I have two boys and I want to leave before someone loses a life. Pray for my children, pray for my husband, pray for me. God bless you. Amen. SEND.

The words traveled into cyberspace as I inhaled through my mouth, filling my chest until I felt my heart being touched. I thought about the billions of bits and bytes it passed just to get to its destination. I looked at the work which was left at my desk. I finished the Excel sheet of my client contacts. I walked to the Executive Director's desk and sat down in front of him.

"Sir, I updated all of the University contacts, there are not many which can be reached by phone. Maybe you should set up a time when we can discuss how they should be contacted."

"I will be leaving for Abuja tomorrow morning, we can talk about it as soon as I get back" he remarked, barely noticing the folder I placed on his desk under some papers.

"Sure," I said as I turned to sit back at my desk.

"Hey Kim, how is Oga?"

I remembered that was the nickname, meaning 'big man,' which he called Steven. "He's well, playing more than ever."

I sat softly in my seat as I began to collect my things quietly and put them in my bag. No one noticed as I lifted the family pictures off the desk.

"Kim, are you feeling well?" Oyin's tiny brown face had a tilt of a smile.

I sat, eyes forward, trying to ignore the fabric that brushed around my legs as she sat beside me. In spite of Oyin's diminutive size, she always carried herself with a dancer's poise. Her dark skin and doe-like eyes always held a glimmer in them. We had grown close in the months we worked together; often spending our lunch hours exchanging cultural practices or dishing over Genevieve magazine's fashion picks.

"I'm ok, just a touch of a head ache. I will be fine once I get home." I placed my hand on top of hers as she walked back to her desk. "Thanks for asking."

A tiny bell signaled an IM at the corner of my computer screen. 'Keep my email address,' smiley face. Log off.

The driver opened the door to the backseat as I tried to conceal my bulky briefcase with the breadth of my open suit jacket.

"Madam, will we be stopping at the market?"

"No, but stop at the roundabout, I want to buy suya for the children."

My thoughts were doing cartwheels in my head as I watched the haze of cars move through traffic.

I gave Ibrahim a few thousand naira and asked him to take the large black gas container to buy some black market diesel for the generator. As soon as he threw his leg over the back seat of the okada I called for the boys. "Malcolm, we are leaving. Please help me with your brother, we don't have much time." He didn't halt his movements, rotating on his back leg; he turned scurrying back down the steps. I opened the door to my closet, reached far towards the back to grab my black pinstriped Versace suit. Touching the inside lining of the suit jacket I located the inside pocket and pulled out three passports. I stuffed each of them between my breast and the wire along the cup of my bra. I took a few steps back to scan my room; the hanging clothes, and those folded neatly on multiple cedar wood racks, the jewelry chest filled with 'bling' and baubles next to the espresso stained dresser, and the countless photo albums under the nightstand next to the bed. I wrote a letter:

When I thought about the love I had for you I based it on countless letters; each one was filled with passion, submission, deep desires, obedience, forgiveness, sacrifice and unconditional love. The words taunted my heart and pierced my soul. It was perfect love with rewards that would outlast our grandchildren's grandchildren passing through the end of time. Each letter was personal. I found the more I read the deeper my understanding of the relationship grew. I stopped writing a long time ago. Every note you have given me you will find in a shoe box under the bed. The letters I refer to were from men I have never met, but they witnessed the love I strived to have. Even through the darkest moments in our relationship they encouraged me to hold on. Your insecurities and jealousies are confirmed, their names: Peter, Paul, Mark and John. I thought this relationship was my cross to bear; funny thing about a cross, it can lead to salvation, or it can be used for crucifixion---I just realized the difference, God has to be in it. He isn't in this. Good bye. Kim

I folded the note, closed it in the Bible and left it on the round black marble table in the sitting area adjacent the bed. I grabbed my purse off the bed and headed downstairs. I noticed the boys had their toy boxes open and large trunk placed in the middle of the room. Clothes lay on top of both of their beds among scattered books and DVDs.

"We aren't taking any luggage. Get whatever you can carry in the next five minutes and we're leaving." Like little soldiers, the boys huddled and progressed through their bedroom and the den. I moved quickly to replace the clothes to their wardrobes and closets. Each DVD, video and book were replaced in their proper place on the shelf. All I could think to grab from their room was the two pictures of them and their daddy which sat on the desk by the window.

Malcolm held his Nintendo Game Cube in one hand, as Steven

hobbled with a back pack full of games slung over one shoulder.

*****

I could feel beads of sweat tracing across my face, skimming down every baby hair until it met my chin. My back was soaked. I could feel every drop of moisture as it slid down the curve of my back to my panties. I could smell the tropical air, the hibiscus and the night smells of suya and oil lanterns. I could smell my fear.

Time took hold of each step that I made. I couldn't move faster. The distance to the end of the steps in the house seemed to descend further. The echoes of Malcolm and Steven's footsteps echoed and blared in my ears, confusing my simplest movements…put one foot in front of the other. I opened the door, pulling before moving the handle. "Go to the taxi, do not make a sound." The boys didn't reply, they just moved. I dropped my cell phone in haste, the back of the frame came off, exposing the battery and the sim card. I set down my address book on my husband's car. I looked for the plastic back, fussing soundlessly, stretching my fingers across the concrete, but the moonlight was not sufficient and each moment brought greater fears. Worried I would miss Gbenga's call and trigger suspicion; I replaced the battery cover and held the phone tightly against the palm of my hand.

The taxi pulled up to the entrance for departing flights. Anguish leaped up my spine as a black Mercedes darted close behind. Three of the four doors opened abruptly as I froze, clenching the boys' little hands.

Relieved, I saw a long pair of legs finished with strappy stilettos hitting the concrete. I glanced at the meter in the taxi, dug into my purse and flung some naira notes at the driver. Feeling deeper into my purse, I felt my Dior sunglasses and fumbled to put them on. We walked to the counter of Virgin Atlantic, my eyes bouncing off faces and fragmented movements. The counter attendant smiled coolly as I handed her our tickets and passports. She asked to have a closer look at the children. I nervously led them to the counter.

"Do we get a pair of wings?" asked Steven, as Malcolm tapped him on the shoulder.

"I will see what I can do for you," she replied, reaching over to hand them two Virgin Atlantic red pins and two colorful draw-string packs. "Will you be paying in naira, dollars or pounds?"

"Pay?" I asked. "I handed you three round trip tickets. What am I paying for?"

"Airport tax. Pounds, dollars or naira?"

I looked in my purse. I had several thousand naira and a twenty dollar bill. I handed her every naira note I had, grabbed our boarding passes, passports, and headed swiftly towards the gate.

We needed to wait out of sight until they called for us to board the plane. My husband knew several people in customs and Airport Authority, and thousands of people traveled through Lagos every day. The women's restroom was not too far from our gate. It might have been hours that passed; it could have been minutes, my blood thundered in my ears.

"Is anyone in here?" the deep tone of a male's voice bellowed.

A bang sounded against the stall beside us. The shadow was approaching. I lifted the boys off the ground and against my body. I held my breath. The figure was getting closer. All of my senses were screaming. I inched closer to the door of the stall. My pulse galloped, my mouth was dry. After several agonizing moments, everything subsided. The threat seemed to pass with a sudden flow of water from the sink and the woosh of the bathroom door.

"Oh, thank God." I sighed.

Crouching with the boys on the cold tiles of the stall, there was a pain inside of me. In the moments my mind was clear, I cursed the times I heard love is blind. I cursed myself wondering if relational glaucoma was hereditary. I thought of the boys trying to catch fish with their hands in the clear water at Takwa Bay, the races they ran up and down the school grounds, the spicy smell of warm suya right out of the paper, every brick laid in 15,000 square feet of living space at our house in the village, or the scent of sweet hibiscus dancing out my window. I thought of everything beautiful I wanted to remember about Nigeria, anything that seemed leagues apart from the violent cyclone which would tear through my life. I looked at Malcolm and Steven, who were holding me close. I took a deep breath for courage. We came out of the stall, turned on the faucet, and waited for the water temperature to get warm so I could splash water over my face.

All passengers traveling to JFK Airport, we will now start preboarding for passengers traveling with small children and those needing assistance.

We approached the Virgin Airways attendant at the gate. She was an attractive round faced ebony woman with skin that appeared the texture of coal. My fingers froze on the edges of the jacket sleeve of the boarding passes, shaking them visibly. I did not remember to pull out our passports. For one awful moment, I looked at her expectant face and thought, *she knows.* I figured they would ask us to step aside. *Where are you taking these children?* She'd say. *Does the father know?* Are you coming back? And then they would take me in a tiny room and make me call Gbenga, while separating the children to ask them several questions.

Swallowing my fear, I smiled mildly and looked the gate agent in the eye. I asked Malcolm to hold his brother's hand. *Remind them you have a return ticket*, I was advised. *Don't sweat, don't panic, and don't travel with visible bruises.* As if I wanted the attention. It was not a badge of honor.

Clearing my throat, I stepped forward. Almost immediately the gate agent moved in front of the jet way, snapping to attention like the changing of the guard at Buckingham Palace. "Good evening," I said, handing her our boarding passes, placing it lightly in her hand.

"Passports?" she asked.

"Oh yes," digging in my purse. "I'm sorry. Right here," I confirmed, handing them to her with the covers opened.

"Thank you ma'am. Have a nice flight home."

I thought her comment sounded absurd, as though back to the States was any more of a home than what I was accustomed to here. I considered how much easier it would have been if I never got attached to Nigeria and the customs. She just left one village to come to another. Gbenga would comment when asked how I fit into Lagos compared to Columbus Ohio. My head was cool; funny it took a singed back to clear that up. This was not going to spoil the way I feel about Nigeria, the people, or my extended family. I kept coming back; even when Gbenga wasn't with me. I may be incidental, but the boys will always be Nigerians.

We walked leisurely passed the gate crew. Looking at the seat numbers displayed prominently on our boarding passes, I was pleased to see we would be sitting together in the middle row. Steven called out the row numbers in sing-song, as we scanned the tags below the luggage compartments. One by one we scooted in the row to take our seats. My heart was still pounding against my rib cage, but I kept a frozen smile while interacting with the boys. I asked both of them to color me a picture using the supplies included in the Virgin Atlantic kid packs- a trick to keep their heads down. As they exchanged crayons back and forth, I read about the kid-TV programs and Nintendo games they could play during the flight.

"Do I have to watch the same thing as he does?" Malcolm asked.

"No. You each have your own TV to look at," the seatback guide answered, trying to cover my face.

As the plane lifted, the scattered insecurities I felt shuffling from my head to my stomach gave way to a serenity that protected and frightened me. Reclining in the seat, I closed my eyes to study it. I reached over to touch the boys on their shoulders. Two handsome strong boys, each one a gift so great that only God himself could have made. I stared out the window at the sprawling city of Lagos, streets twinkling with clusters of lights in the go-slow morph into silver white eyes winking at me from the sky.

Light is breaking through the cabin. The plane windows are glazed peach, the cabin still with cool, dry air, its passengers mostly sleeping. I looked up at the screen as the in flight movie concluded. The seat-back monitor displayed the flight finder map. I wasn't sure what I would find when I got there, but I knew in order to get somewhere, the first step was to leave.

If you allow someone to get to that love inside of you, before you find it for yourself, then you will find a mix of rebellion and submission which will make you lose your sense of direction and purpose. I found my direction.

First Corinthians, chapter 13

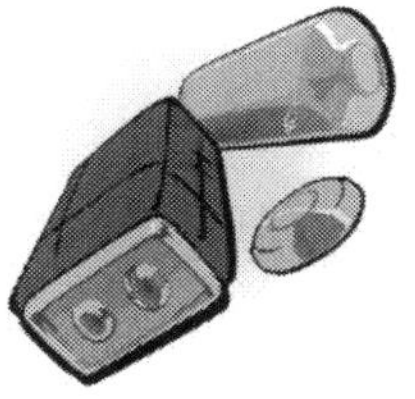

I haven't been BATTERED, I've been BATTERIED

List and Listen (Confront your anxieties)

Make a list of what's holding you back from taking the risk (challenges & strengths)

Make a list of when you were brave; list your 'out of the box' moments that turned out great

You will see you have overcome before and recognize where you are strong. Use those strengths to get you through.

Get Centered

If you never saw it coming, you were probably distracted. There are

ALWAYS signs. Get calm, be still and get focused.

Make Your Own Change

The best way to cope with change is to create it YOURSELF. If you allow other people to dictate the change for you, you are reacting in defense. Make your own offense.

Hold onto FAITH

Your lowest moment can be your best moment. Your darkest time can be what makes you shine. It is in those times you really learn about yourself and what you are made of. Once you know what you are capable of, it can never be taken from you.

Made in the USA
Charleston, SC
12 April 2011